PENGUIN CLASSICS

LI PO *and* TU FU

LI PO (or LI T'AI–PO) and TU FU are seen by the Chinese as the two greatest poets of an age that to them, like our Renaissance, links the ancient with the modern world. The two poets were contemporaries and friends and shared a deep love of the poetry of the past, but were widely different in their own character and work. Yet they complemented one another so well that they came often to be spoken of as one, 'Li-Tu', who, more than any single poet, covered the whole range of human nature.

LI PO (A.D. 701–62) was born in the far west of China, and probably had some knowledge of Central Asian languages and cultures. But to his contemporaries his talent was almost supernatural, so that he hardly seemed of earthly origin at all; his verses seemed to originate in something other than the human consciousness, yet speak directly and simply to the human mind.

TU FU (A.D. 712–70) was born near the capital, of a family distinguished for service to the state. While Li Po seems to the Chinese to be a poet of the night and of man as a solitary animal in his dreams, Tu Fu is rather a poet of the day and of man in his other nature as a social animal. Tu Fu's poems chronicle his life and times with social conscience and compassion, but also present a convincing, unselfconscious portrait of the man himself.

SHUI CHEIN-TUNG, artist and scholar, who has contributed calligraphy to this book, was, like Li Po, born in the far west of China. He is co-author with Bernard Martin of *Makers of China* (1972).

ARTHUR COOPER who was born in 1916 of Anglo-Irish parents and as a boy explored foreign languages and poetry, starting with Icelandic, later turning to Japanese and Chinese. He entered the Foreign Office in 1938, served in Hong Kong and Singapore 1939–42, and for several years in Australia under the British High Commission. He retired in 1968 and devoted himself to the Chinese language, especially the script, and poetry. In 1978 he published a monograph on *The Creation of the Chinese Script*, seeing a new look at this subject as important to the understanding of the earliest Chinese literature, especially poetry, and also to that of the evolution of human language. He died in 1988.

LI PO *AND* TU FU

POEMS SELECTED AND TRANSLATED
WITH AN INTRODUCTION AND NOTES
BY
ARTHUR COOPER

CHINESE CALLIGRAPHY
BY
SHUI CHIEN-TUNG

PENGUIN BOOKS

PENGUIN BOOKS

Published by the Penguin Group
Penguin Books Ltd, 27 Wrights Lane, London W8 5TZ, England
Penguin Books USA Inc., 375 Hudson Street, New York, New York 10014, USA
Penguin Books Australia Ltd, Ringwood, Victoria, Australia
Penguin Books Canada Ltd, 10 Alcorn Avenue, Toronto, Ontario, Canada M4V 3B2
Penguin Books (NZ) Ltd, 182–190 Wairau Road, Auckland 10, New Zealand

Penguin Books Ltd, Registered Offices: Harmondsworth, Middlesex, England

First published 1973
11 13 15 17 19 20 18 16 14 12

Set in Bembo Monotype
Printed in England by Clays Ltd, St Ives plc

FOR DIANA

CONTENTS

ACKNOWLEDGEMENTS

To many friends I am deeply grateful for encouragement and for enduring being shown successive drafts of poems; particularly to Elisabeth Ayrton, Michael Alexander (who gave me 'glee'), Paul Wilkinson (also for the gift of a superb old edition of Tu Fu), Betty Radice, Harold and Barbara Ryder; and to my neighbours Bob Bass and Roderick Snell, Philip and Angela Lowery. I am grateful further for generous expert advice, drawing my attention to and lending me books, and more, to Professor David Hawkes, Oxford, and to Professor Denis Twitchett, Dr Michael Loewe, Dr Paul Kratochvil and Wing Commander Bob Sloss, Cambridge; and both for the music and for a most helpful and delightful correspondence, to Dr Laurence Picken. Mistakes, however, and mistaken ideas are all my own. To Shui Chientung I am deeply indebted for the beauty of his calligraphy, for encouragement, and also for never directly instructing me, as he might well have done, but for letting his own imaginative and stimulating thoughts *ricochet* helpfully about the work; like the most enjoyable Taoist 'teaching without words'. To my brother Joshua Cooper I owe thoughts about language everywhere silently purloined; and to my wife, to whom this book is dedicated, I owe the rest.

Cranham, Gloucester   A.R.V.C.
1971

PRONUNCIATION OF CHINESE WORDS AND NAMES

THE romanization in this book is the still most generally used 'Wade-Giles' system:

Consonants

The apostrophe after a consonant, as in *p'ing*, represents a strong breath. It is best to pronounce such consonants like an English 'p' (etc.) but to pronounce those without the apostrophe as 'b' (etc.): for example *t'ing* as 'ting' but *ting* as 'ding'; *ch'ing* as 'ching' but *ching* as 'jing'.

The romanized letter *j* is pronounced in Pekinese (which this romanization otherwise represents) like an English unrolled 'r'; for example *ju* as the English word 'rue'. (The supposed Chinese inability to say 'r' applies to other dialects.) *Hs*- at the beginning of a word is between the sound in 'hew' and the sound in 'sue': *hsü*.

Vowels

ü is like German 'ü' or French 'u'. *Hsüeh*, *yüeh* nearly rhyme with French 'tué' but the

-eh is like the English 'e' in 'get'. (The final *h* in this romanization is a convention and never pronounced.)

e on its own is the neutral vowel in English 'err'. If the 'r' in this word is pronounced fully, it is like the Chinese word romanized as *erh*.

-ih is a vocalic 'r': *shih* is like 'shr' as some Americans pronounce 'sure'.

-u in *szu, tzu* is a vocalic 'z': 'szz, dzz'. *Ts'z* is 'tszz'.

ao is the English sound in 'cow'.

ei is the English sound in 'way', 'day'.

ie is 'ee-eh'.

ou is the English sound in 'though', 'go'.

o on its own is the English sound in 'thaw', but sometimes neutralized to an 'er' sound. (When neutral, *e* and *o* are sometimes written *ê* and *ô*.)

'a', 'i', 'u' on their own are as in Italian. Subject to observance, only as far as convenient, of these rough indications of Chinese pronunciation, it is best to pronounce the romanizations in an English way: e.g. *Wang* as 'Wong', *Chuang Chou* as 'Jwong Joe'.

Some names, like Szechwan (*Szu-ch'uan*) and Peking (*Pei-ching*), I spell in the most usual way; and I prefer to pronounce *Li Po* and *Tu Fu* themselves as English 'Lee Poe' and 'Too Foo,' instead of with 'Baw' and 'Doo'.

NOTE ON THE CHINESE CALLIGRAPHY

THERE was a great deal of variety in the drawing of Chinese characters before 'spelling reforms' of the 3rd century B.C. The abolition then of the feudal states and the establishment of a central bureaucracy made the standardization of the drawing of the characters both necessary and possible. Two scripts, both surviving for occasional formal use in book-titles and the like, were then devised within a few years of one another: the 'Lesser Seal' or 'Simplified Formal' script and the *Li* or 'Police' script. The latter was the first Chinese writing designed specially for the writing brush, which was swift because it was almost frictionless; and in it the curves of earlier writing are replaced by angles better suited to a brush.

All later styles of Chinese writing are modifications of the 'Li' script, with curves returning, largely as ligatures, in the most rapid forms. These later styles developed with the invention of paper, ideal for brush and ink, in the 2nd century A.D.; whilst the invention of printing, about the 9th century, had other influences on the forms of the script.

The paper on which the Chinese paint, write and print is much softer, however, and more absorbent than our printing paper, and the method of printing they invented uses a lighter contact between paper and inked matrix than our later invention of the printing press. The Chinese method is more sympathetic to a calligrapher's handiwork with brush and water-based ink.

To suit our paper and press, Mr Shui has therefore adopted a manner influenced by Chinese bronze inscriptions in his transcribing of the texts of some of the poems translated in this book. In doing so he has also followed various styles of writing to suit the different poems, as is commonly done in Chinese calligraphy; but he has not made historical faithfulness to the forms in these styles his principal aim, in which he also follows the traditions of Chinese calligraphy, especially calligraphy by painters – the spirit in the calligraphic art always counting for more than the form.

INTRODUCTION

1. 'Li-Tu'

KENNETH CLARK in *Civilisation* remarks:

Great men have a curious way of appearing in complementary pairs. This has happened so often in history that I don't think it can have been invented by symmetrically-minded historians, but must represent some need to keep human faculties in balance.

To the Chinese the two poets of this book, Li Po (also called Li T'ai-po), A.D. 701–62, and Tu Fu (also called Tu Tzu-mei, Tu Shao-ling and Tu Kung-pu), A.D. 712–70, make such a pair and are also generally regarded as their greatest poets. Chinese thought would agree, too, that such pairs 'must represent some need to keep human faculties in balance': a balance they saw from early times throughout Nature and called the Yang and the Yin.

These were originally topographical terms, like 'shine' and 'shade': Yang for the south side of a hill, the north bank of a river, the sun itself, and the male sex, among other things; and Yin for the north side of a hill, the south bank of a river, the moon and planets that reflect the sun's light, and the female sex, among other things. This does not mean that every such complementary pair as Lord Clark is thinking of, for instance Bach and Handel who occasioned his remark, can be thought of as one belonging to Yin and the other to Yang; because a healthy living being in the ancient Chinese ideas which created the notion (and included all Creation, rocks, earth and sky among living beings) is made up of both

15

elements harmoniously balanced, even though one of them may in some way be in the lead. Although a man was Yang for his sex, and a woman Yin for hers, this did not mean that they should be all-Yang or all-Yin respectively without possessing within themselves the proper harmonious balance.

Such a balance was part of the great Way, *Tao* in Chinese, of Nature; of which Man himself in all his activities was part. Ancient Chinese thinking, extending to the great philosophers, was therefore based on the assumption of a single Tao which included both natural science and moral philosophy.

There was, however, a Yang way and a Yin way of imagining this Tao. The Yang way, which belonged to what came to be called the Confucian school of thought when Confucius (551–479 B.C.) became accepted as its leading ancient sage, regarded the Tao as something that could be illumined, by etiquette, ritual and music as well as by words, for the benefit of good individual and social morality; and so also of good government, which all the early Chinese philosophers saw as the primary concern of philosophy, their personal ambitions being to achieve posts as political advisers to rulers.

The principal opposing school of thought was given the name of Taoist, although both parties equally accepted the notion of the Tao and the belief that if it were only found and followed then it would be possible for the best government to be the least government; 'without action', as they called it. Lao Tzu, the legendary ancient sage of the Taoists who was made out to be an older contemporary of Confucius (to enable them to argue), said that a great country should be governed as one would cook a small fish, that is, not pulling it about; but Confucius himself would have agreed with this view. Where they differed was that the Taoists took a Yin view of the Tao: that it was such that any illumination of it, as sought for in the Yang outlook of the Confucians, would only make it disappear; just as a spot of reflected light on a dark surface disappears when another light is shone on it. To live individually and socially the good life in accordance with the Tao, and to govern in accordance with it, one must therefore on no account try to illumine it with one's own intellect, still less suppose that anything could be learned about the Tao by arguing about it. The Taoists' teaching must instead be 'without words'; that is to say, although they might in fact use as many words as did the Confucians in expounding their philosophy, they would never make the mistake (as they regarded it) of supposing that words could convey anything *itself* useful about the Tao, rather than merely act as reflecting surfaces for the Tao's own light.

To the Confucians, therefore, much of Taoist teaching seemed childishly irrelevant to any practical affairs, even downright dotty. (Ch'an, or by its Japanese pronunciation Zen, Buddhism is essentially a Chinese grafting, dating from the sixth century after Christ, of their ancient Taoism on to the imported Indian religion.) To the Taoists, on the other hand, the Confucians were naïve in supposing that they could construct models of the Tao by the light of their own intellects, and it was inevitable that any such models would only be false and harmful. The Taoists were right, insofar as it was their Yin way of looking on the Tao that contributed most to Chinese progress in natural science,* to which the Confucian Yang view like our own theological dogma

*See various works on Chinese science by Dr Joseph Needham; especially Volume 2 of his great *Science and Civilisation in China.*

in the Middle Ages was, more often than not, an impediment; but they were wrong, insofar as they allowed themselves, by contrast, to be dogmatically anarchistic in their political notions of the way to the good government, on which human liberty depends and to which the Confucians made by far the better contribution.

To a hard-headed and down-to-earth people such as the Chinese have always been, it has always been obvious (even though neither philosophic party might explicitly agree) that no man could be entirely a Confucian or entirely a Taoist in his attitude to this essential Tao but every man must be a bit of both, just as he himself is made up of elements of both Yang and Yin. A passion for consistency has never been one of the major Chinese passions, and it has been a happy thing for them that their most discussed conflict of thought should have been over something that could never (like there being only one God) even seem to be absolute; for it probably set the way for the Chinese among all the great civilizations of the world to have by far the best record, even if not altogether unblemished, in the matter of religious toleration.

As a member of Society, in the daytime going to work, earning his living, paying his debts, respecting the old, bringing up the young, every man must make use of a great deal of Confucian illumination of the Tao; but he must also liberate himself at times, as an individual, from all this and escape from what would be called his real problems together with their potentially illumined solutions; letting the light of the Tao itself be reflected in his dreams at night, which are no less part of his life and of his humanity.

Li Po is the Taoist in this pair of poets, and his constantly recurring symbol is the reflected light of the

Moon at night; whilst Tu Fu is the Confucian who from early childhood made the Phoenix his symbol, the Fire Bird symbolizing the Yang.

It is true and fair therefore to accuse Li Po of being an escapist: he has helped provide the healing of escape to his countrymen for twelve centuries; sometimes making them forget their problems in unthinking gaiety, but still more making them feel (by stimulating, as it were, their *peripheral* rather than their *direct* vision) that there is infinitely more in the Universe than what is worrying them, or than they can see directly and understand. Not surprisingly, Li Po has often been severely condemned for this escapism; by some Confucians and now by some Communists. Yet Tu Fu, whose life and work showed at their best all the Confucian virtues of humanity and humility (with which also goes a sense of humour!), was not only the older poet's devoted friend but had the deepest understanding, sympathy and admiration for his work; and, though himself a moralist, never, unlike most of even the friendliest critics of Li Po, even hints at moral disapprobation of the life he led.

It seems a pity therefore that these two are sometimes categorized, one to be treated sympathetically at the expense of the other, in ways to create a conflict between them that never existed and that they would not have understood. Many people seem always to have thought that their own advocacy of the one could only be improved by condemning the other: Li Po as irresponsibly amoral, careless in versification and insufficiently serious; or Tu Fu as narrowly moral, rigid in versification and excessively serious.

The selection of translated poems in this book, though with great loss in quantity as well as quality compared with what both poets left (26 poems for each, whereas

19

Li Po left about 1,000 and Tu Fu about 1,400), may reveal their characters better than such generalized judgements; and show why later T'ang poets, despite the contrasts between them, made them one: 'Li-Tu'.

2. The Background to their Times

The age in which these poets lived has ever since been regarded as the most golden of all the golden ages in the 3,000 years (five times as long as between Chaucer and ourselves) of Chinese poetry; a poetry which has (because of the nature of the language and its script, as will be seen later in this Introduction) a continuity of tradition unknown in any other of the world's literatures.

The China of Confucius and the other philosophers, of small fiefs whose rulers they endeavoured to guide, had disappeared nearly a thousand years earlier; to be replaced by a unified Empire roughly contemporary with the period of greatness of the Roman Republic and Empire, before the Roman partition into East and West. This had been followed in China, too, by partition of the Empire (in the third century after Christ) and by barbarian invasions; a time sometimes called 'the Chinese Dark Ages' but, despite political upheaval, one also of great intellectual and artistic activity inspired by influences from abroad. The most important of these was undoubtedly Buddhism, received from India, and with it the recognition that the Chinese was not after all the only civilization in the world. (There had earlier been little more than rumours of distant Greece and Rome.)

Then, at the end of the sixth century, the Empire was unified again under the short-lived Sui dynasty. This was nevertheless one of the great foundation-laying periods of Chinese history. There were extraordinary achievements in the organization of administration, including consolidation of an earlier, imperfect examination system to ensure that merit was the chief way to power in governing the Empire. (This was something which, surviving little changed in the nineteenth century, was to influence the establishment of our own Civil Service Examinations.)

There were also no less extraordinary achievements in engineering, the building of canals, dykes, roads and bridges. Despite all this progress, the fundamental weakness of the Empire, however, remained (and was to remain throughout its history up to this century). It was still a despotism, even if to some extent 'constitutionalized' in practice by the existence of a powerful Confucian bureaucracy; and its fate therefore was greatly dependent on the character of the despot, subject even to change as a result of senility or disease, so that his mere whims could affect the lives of millions. The second ruler of the Sui dynasty was licentious, extravagant and cruel, and the dynasty was brought down by rebellion.

The Chinese had always accepted an important qualification to the Divine Right of Kings, namely the notion of the Mandate of Heaven which could be withdrawn at such times and bestowed on a successful revolutionary. The revolutionary in this case was the famous Li Shih-min, 597–649, who, though out of filial piety he first put his father on the throne before assuming it himself as the Emperor T'ai-tsung, was the real founder of the great T'ang dynasty, 618–906. The age that now began was at least until very recently treated by the Chinese as the beginning of Modern Times (their Middle Ages dating from the beginning of the Empire in the third century B.C.). It was an age of relative stability of government, at least compared with anything known in nearby centuries, and of prosperity in the national economy; also of virility of indigenous culture, inspired and assisted, not damaged, by foreign influences which were welcomed wholeheartedly by a once again united and confident people.

About a century passed, however, before the T'ang arts began to catch up with the other progress of that age; the poetry, for instance, of the seventh century being little different in technique or range from that of the preceding century. The early part of the eighth century was a time of an extraordinary freshness of outlook and of even greater peace and prosperity, in which new arts could flourish; owed largely to a wholly unique episode in Chinese history, shortly before. This was the rule of the great Empire by a brilliant and tight-fisted woman, the Empress Wu (625–705), who had been a young concubine of the ageing Emperor T'ai-tsung, and reigned from 684 in fact and in name from 690.* An age in which such an extraordinary thing could have happened was indeed a new age; in addition to which, her tight-fistedness, like that of Henry VII at the beginning of our own Tudor times, which the times of these poets in many ways resembled, laid the foundations of its prosperity and arts.

3. Li Po

Although nowhere near as fortunate in that respect as Shakespeare, not a great deal is really known about the life of Li Po.† Even the place of his birth, information

* There is a biography, *The Empress Wu*, by C. P. Fitzgerald (Cheshire, Melbourne, 1955); author also of the admirable *China: A Short Cultural History* (Cresset Press, 1935, with many reprintings).

† Arthur Waley, however, says surprisingly 'Li Po is one of the Chinese poets about whose life we know most'; but must rather mean

regularly made available in the most minor Chinese biographies, and its date have been, at least until recently, the subjects of much speculation. This seems all the more curious in view of his exceptional fame in his own lifetime; but it is now generally agreed that he was born in 701 and outside present-day China, probably near what is now the frontier of the Soviet Union and Afghanistan. The name of his original home would therefore have meant very little to his contemporaries, who must be excused also for not knowing his place of birth because he spent most of his life travelling and had the romantic habit of speaking of many places he particularly liked as if they were his own home. (There had probably never before been such facilities for tourism, and safety in it; for which Tu Fu, when opportunity allowed, was no less enthusiastic.) Furthermore Li Po, having been praised for his extraordinary talent in early youth as a 'Fallen Immortal' or 'Banished Fairy', was inclined for ever after to adopt this character; to which a fixed earthly abode would have been unsuitable.

Also, though like other poets of his time he wrote many occasional poems, parting from friends, thanking for hospitality and the like, these do not generally contain much information useful for biography; while his major poems, being for the most part dream poems, are seldom informative about the time or circumstances in which they were written. In this they are in marked contrast with those of Tu Fu, which are almost all to some extent historical and autobiographical; so that

---

'about whom there is the most gossip'. This is in *The Poetry and Career of Li Po* (Allen and Unwin, 1950), a rather unsympathetic study, that one cannot help suspecting was written partly to justify the great translator's often expressed personal lack of appreciation of this poet.

scholarship has been able to date most of these with remarkable precision, better even than for some of our own poets a thousand years later.

Therefore, although Tu Fu's poems are arranged chronologically in this book and serve as a frame for a biography of him and a history of the times of both poets, no such attempt is made for Li Po's poems; this despite confident but highly contradictory dating of them, based on wisps of evidence, by some affectionate Chinese scholars. There is a very ancient Confucian literary tradition that would make *all* poetry occasional and moral; and so to be understood properly only in relation to the circumstances of its inspiration, preferably of a political nature. The difficulty found by many Chinese scholars, who nevertheless cannot help loving him, of fitting Li Po into this frame has often been a painful embarrassment to them.

Li Po's family tradition was that an ancestor of about a century earlier had been banished for political reasons, if not at first to the place of the poet's own birth then to some other outlandish Western Region; and that this ancestor was himself a descendent of the autonomous Duke, Li Kao (d. A.D. 417), of a region in what is now Kansu Province in West China. The latter was also claimed as ancestor by the Imperial Family of Li Shih-min who had founded the T'ang dynasty, so that Li Po felt able to address Imperial Princes as 'cousins'. Farther back still, Li Kao was known to be a descendent of General Li Kuang (d. 125 B.C.), a famous scourge of the Huns who had called him 'The Flying General'; and yet farther back, in common with all families of this Li surname, including of course the Imperial Family who favoured Taoism for that reason, they claimed descent from one Li Erh, who was supposed to have been the historical Lao Tzu ('Old Sage') himself in the sixth century B.C.; but this last was undoubtedly mythical.

Against this romantic ancestry, a dark suspicion must be mentioned that Li Po's family were not even Chinese at all, but Turks. That both they and the Imperial Li Family, along with many other leading families of the Empire, had some Turkish connections may be taken as certain; but as far as Li Po's own family is concerned, it is of greater significance than any 'blood' that they had lived for several generations in Turkish-speaking parts (Li Po himself said he could compose poetry in 'another language', probably some form of Turkish) and, like many an Anglo-Irish family without ever a 'Mac' or an 'O' in its ancestry, may even have chosen in some respects to go 'more Turkish than the Turks'. One son of the Glorious Monarch (reigned 713–56), obsessed by the Turkishness of the Imperial Family, certainly did this and vacated his palace to live in a tent in his garden.

To be Chinese at that date, however, was, playful fantasies apart, to acknowledge the Emperor's Mandate from Heaven and to be literate in Chinese. By these, the only real criteria, Li Po was certainly Chinese to all his contemporaries. Whatever his true ancestry and however much he may have chosen in a cosmopolitan, outward-looking age to let Turkish, Persian and other foreign influences affect his art, these foreign influences were affecting in various ways all the Chinese arts of his time, without a suspicion of the artists themselves being 'alien'.

To suggest further, as has been done, that his notorious drunkenness was an inherited 'barbarian' trait is certainly beside the point in an age when, among specially talented people, drunkenness was universally recognized as a state of perfect, untramelled receptivity to divine inspiration; with no hint of Turkishness or anything 'barbaric' about it. (A similar view has also, of course, prevailed at times in our own civilization, notably in the Greek Mysteries and the Bacchic or Dionysiac state of ecstasy.) In all, there seems no reason at all to attribute anything in Li Po's character or work to 'foreign blood'.

Li Po's family had come and settled in China proper, in the south-western province of Szechwan, by the time he was five years old, so he is unlikely to have had much direct memory of an exotic past. It is probable, however, that in the remote regions the family had been traders, and that they kept up with foreign trading communities of all races and religions (Zoroastrian, Hindu, Jewish, Nestorian Christian, Muslim) then to be found all over China; and as represented by the obviously un-Chinese-looking figures often found in T'ang pottery. If they were themselves traders in a China dominated by a professional class of civil servants, they would (even if rich) not quite have been 'gentry'; but however Chinese or aristocratic their origins may in fact have been, they would anyway not have belonged to the local 'landed gentry' wherever they settled. Such circumstances could have contributed to a number of things: their concern and his with a supposed grand ancestry (Tu Fu, whose ancestry really was grand, says nothing about it); the combination, which helped to make Li Po's work so striking to his contemporaries, of evident foreign influences with equally strong and self-conscious Chinese tradition, but looking back to a distant Chinese past more than to recent movements and fashions; and the un-Confucian, that is to say, not quite gentlemanly, boastfulness and competitiveness of character that he displayed. This background could also help explain his constant wandering; and the great loneliness to be found in all his work, despite his outward high spirits and success. No man was ever more recognized for his genius in his lifetime.

Li Po was not merely un-Confucian in his manners, enjoying or hiding himself in a reputation as an *enfant terrible*, but often explicitly anti-Confucian in his thought. He poured scorn on the moral and intellectual qualities (such as patient literary scholarship) most admired in the Confucian tradition, and expressed his own admiration only for the man of impulse. For a time in his youth he lived as a wandering gallant, whose sword was free to redress wrongs wherever he went.* In this character he seems to have had something in common with Cyrano de Bergerac: both the real seventeenth-century man, with his free-thinking, his imaginary journeys to the sun and moon, and his serious studies of physics; and the theatrical one of Rostand's play. Nothing, however, is known of Li Po's prowess (he only says, in a prose letter, that he was keen on swordsmanship at the age of fifteen) or of his achievements in this kind of life. But he is said by contemporaries to have killed several men.

Neither these adventures, however, which certainly did not continue far into his life, nor his drunkenness which did, nor even his satirizing of Confucian virtues (an accepted sport of the time, played also on occasion by Tu Fu who, by his own account, was a heavy drinker, too) — none of these things has been so shocking ever since to the Confucian outlook as Li Po's refusal, despite the outstanding talents early evident in his poetic compositions, to take the official examinations and serve the

* This was an old Chinese tradition, found also in Japan and the subject of a number of famous Japanese stories and now films. There is an excellent and scholarly history and description of it in China, in James J. Y. Liu's *The Chinese Knight Errant* (Routledge and Kegan Paul, 1967).

Empire in its higher civil service. Poetic genius most of all, but also the other higher arts such as calligraphy, painting and music, which were distinguished from mere crafts, meant in the traditional Chinese view an understanding of the single Tao, such as would be wasted if not given also in other ways to the service of Empire and of people. An ivory tower was suitable to poets only when preparing themselves for such service; or after it, to retreat to nobly instead of accepting wealth and honour; or sometimes when grievously wronged while in service; or for religious ascetics, who might also be poets and, if good enough, should also then be considered for such service.

There have been various speculations about why Li Po did not take the examinations. Perhaps pride was a reason, given uncertainty of coming out first in the list: an acceptable reason, for such pride was fully respected in a brilliant youth of this Renaissance-like age. There was a further excuse because this was before examination papers were handed in on completion with ciphers instead of names, so that influence still counted. But Li Po might have obtained such influence, and none of this could be a lasting excuse. Perhaps he was simply too impulsive and incapable of the necessary self-discipline to get through all the preparation with set books and model questions on government and economics. There is evidence, however, that he was very widely read, spent much of his life in study, and by no means lacked the kind of ambitions for which it was normally necessary to take the examinations.

Among subjects he studied on his own account (and incorporated in his poetry) was what would now be called physics and chemistry. This may point to another reason why, so disconcertingly to his admirers then and since, he did not take the examinations: he might have taken them if the curriculum had been in anything but arts subjects, drawn up by Confucians, with which he was impatient and the relevance of which he did not see. Although his chemistry may have been directed at such things as finding 'elixirs of life', the imagination in his poetry seems essentially one of 'natural philosophy', and as such quite different from Tu Fu's.

Politically, in fact, he remained (like some scientists) always a child; and this political naïvety of his has led to his being charged with lack of concern for the welfare of the people, with being selfish and without compassion in contrast to Tu Fu, especially during the turbulent age which theirs (after beginning in such peace and prosperity) was to become during their lives.* That the charge is not altogether just may be seen from some of the poems in this book. Li Po in his own way possessed great sympathy and compassion for his fellow-beings (including an especially sympathetic insight into the minds of women) and was fiercely indignant at all suffering of which he was aware, for instance in war. But he can also give a fatalistic impression because he had little notion of practical solutions; or (again like some scientists) was inclined to regard everybody else's stupidity as the self-evident explanation of all evil. It was enough to see that something was not in harmony with the Tao, and difficult then to take any further interest in it. That, with his impulsiveness and all else in his character (including, I think, an incapability of expecting to be misunderstood, which gives his poems their special spontaneity) was all part of his Taoism.

*Little of what he wrote in this later time may have survived, judging by a statement of a cousin of his that nine out of ten of all his last works were lost.

It was also part of his Taoism that his poems seem to receive rather than to give: to receive the light of the Tao without illumination of their own and to receive, hospitably, the reader's own imagination instead of informing it. The real content of Li Po's best poetry seems to be not in the words but as if it were somehow in-between them (Lao Tzu's 'teaching without words'); as in the five simple syllables, with those italicized added for English grammar: 'drunk*enly I* rise *to* stalk *the* brook moon'. Li Po has dozed over his wine outdoors in spring until night has fallen: that much we have been told. That the stream he followed on waking and getting up from the ground (there is no harm in imagining a chair, though in China in those days people seldom sat on them) ran between magical wooded slopes, we are not told; and these wooded slopes are made the more magical, their presence is the more felt, *because* we are not told. We are therefore *there*, just as we are where we are now; with nobody telling us where we are or *describing* what is around us.

We know, in fact, by two things that there are wooded slopes: that the moon belongs only to the brook and not also to its banks, as it would if they were open fields; and that it has to be 'stalked', which is a reasonable translation of the Chinese verb used. But we have no need to think in this logical way and no time to do so, before being taken from wherever we may be and placed in that faraway landscape and at that moment more than twelve hundred years ago; bringing nothing but ourselves with us on the flight and so achieving perfect identity with the man Li Po, there and then.

This kind of technique, which is not often subject to such rational analysis as attempted here, belongs, of course, in varying degrees and among other techniques to all the best poetry in the world. But the Chinese language, for reasons which will be seen when we come to discuss it, is particularly suited to it; and Li Po seems to use it with exceptional spontaneity and skill, especially in the very short form of poem of which he is universally acknowledged one of the greatest masters. It not only contributes to the extraordinary visual quality of much Chinese poetry, his in particular, far more than any explicit description could do: it leads to very simple yet profound thoughts, as part of a time and place, such as may never be thought in words at all and can hardly be expressed in them without banality. These are thoughts which, like the Tao itself in the Taoist imagination of it, disappear on illumination.

Unfortunately for the translator, poetry of this kind uses everything in a poem to make a texture, as it were, in order to catch the wavelength of the Tao that it seeks; so that it is even less transferrable than other kinds of poetry from the texture of its own language into another. But if one is at first half-inclined to react to translations of some of these very simple little Chinese poems (also the Japanese equivalent) with a 'So what?', so, it must be admitted, one may often be inclined at first, on reading them in the original: they *do* have very little to say, but even in translation (in which so much of their reflective surface is usually dulled) they may sometimes be found to have a correspondingly great amount to *reflect*. It is because of this that at their best they are infinitely re-readable, never losing their freshness; so that a very short poem may come to seem a great one.

Besides these very short poems and some that are longer but similar in spirit and technique, Li Po is most famous for poems in old ballad styles, called *yüeh-fu*. These may be described as quasi-folksongs. In fact,

31

they have much deeper thought and learning than folk-songs but use the folksong model both for its music (to which these poems were sung)* and for its tradition, like that of folksongs and ballads all over the world, of allowing quick jumps in time and space and mood, and of avoiding the explicit. The name *yüeh-fu*, often translated 'Music Bureau', derives from the name of a musical academy established in 90 B.C. for collecting folksongs, among other purposes. This was seen in the Confucian tradition as a way of discovering the mind of the people: their needs and aspirations, and their feelings about the government they enjoyed or endured.

Although this academy did not exist for very long, it had a profoundly beneficial influence in after ages for the tradition it created of recording the words of ballads and folksongs, and for counteraction against excessively erudite and rule-bound 'classical' tendencies in a poetry produced by a social class chosen mainly by literary examination.

In much of Li Po's versification he was antiquarian rather than either conservative or modernist. He preferred generally the older, freer metres ungoverned by recently developed rules (rather like those of Malherbe in sixteenth-century France). These new rules served to counterpoint the intrinsic tones of words (as described further below) and were exploited with great effect by Tu Fu. Li Po, however, was often better suited by the very irregular lengths of line in some of the old *yüeh-fu* and by the uninterrupted runs of strong syllables (rather like G. M. Hopkins' 'dappled dawn drawn falcon') that could occur in them; and he seems also to have been

* Other poems were chanted rather than said, usually to the accompaniment of a zither. There was no notion of reading poems silently till perhaps a thousand years later.

more of a spontaneous, natural singer (with such echoes in his mental ear) than a conscious theorist and experimenter as was Tu Fu.

Poetry in the West since the eighteenth century has tended to move from 'rules' to 'freedom', so that one might get an impression that of these two Li Po was more the 'modern poet'; but in their own day it was the other way round. Tu Fu was more the innovator, and it was he who made the typically 'avant-garde' remark in one of his poems: 'Until death I shall not rest, to make my words startle men!' Li Po nevertheless was also a 'discoverer', particularly of little noticed or remembered poets of earlier centuries; such as one Yin K'eng, who lived some time in the sixth century, significantly also in the Western Regions, and whose few surviving verses have a Li Po vigour and mystery.

Li Po's ear was also without a doubt informed by the 'urban pop music' of his day, in places with food, wine and cabaret, which were the contemporary equivalent of night clubs. Many of the girls in these places were foreign and brought new kinds of song and dance from Central Asia.* That the nomadic peoples of this vast area were largely without writing did not mean that they were without culture or that their music was primitive. (Music has had perhaps much more power as a messenger between civilizations than it is generally credited with: Turkish fifes and drums and songs may have carried the seeds of new thought in both directions from one literate civilization to another, even though they had no literate communication, across the mountain ranges and deserts between them.) New Chinese

* 'Pop' of this kind seems always to have been the origin of new Chinese verse-forms; including, half a millennium earlier, the classical five- and seven-syllable metres of Li Po's and Tu Fu's own day.

verse-forms, called *tz'u*, for singing to the new popular music and allowing irregular lengths of line to fit the tunes, had their origin at this time, though their own 'classical' age was in the tenth to the thirteenth centuries.*

The tune of one of these songs of the T'ang dynasty survives thanks to a twelfth-century musician and poet, Chiang K'uei, who discovered it from an old lutenist at an inn in Nankin in 1198 and printed it with his own words in a song-book in 1202. (The songs usually went out of fashion from generation to generation, surviving only as verse-metres.) With the very kind permission of Dr Laurence Picken of Jesus College, Cambridge, who transcribed it from its old Chinese notation, this beautiful little melody is reproduced below; with a syllable-for-syllable translation I have attempted of the lyric composed to it by Chiang K'uei. Although not by Li Po, this short song seems to have clear affinities with some of the songs translated here; and may therefore, with its music, bring these and the spirit of the age to which he belonged nearer to the reader.

The song is of a girl of the *geisha* kind to her departing noble lover.

ANCIENT AIR FOR THE LUTE

又　正　是　春　歸　細　柳　暗
And　so　now　Spring　ends　Wil-lows weave

*See *A Collection* and *A Further Collection of Chinese Lyrics* by Alan Ayling and Duncan Mackintosh (Routledge & Kegan Paul, 1965 and 1969).

34

黄 千 縷　暮 鴉　啼 廒
yel - low strands,　Cry - evening crows:

夢 逐 金 鞍 去　一 點 芳
Your gold sad - dle - bow　Dreams not words

心 不 訴　琵 琶 解 語
fol - low now: Those my lute knows!*

Li Po may be called a 'romantic' poet in that almost all his poems are to some extent dream-poems; many of his longer ones spirit-journeys, for which he had precedents in ancient poems related to the trances of mediums in early Chinese religious dances. (Coleridge's *Kubla Khan* is, of course, such a spirit-journey; and more will be said of it concerning a poem of Li Po's which has some affinities with it.) Some scholars who quite approve of such spirit-journeys and find them moving, given that they are in the setting of a 'primitive' society with 'interesting' customs and ways

*The second verse is more literally: 'Dreams follow your gold saddle, there is a little sweetness my heart does not put into words: my lute understands the language (for that).' Chinese can express such an idea in far fewer words and syllables than English.

of thought ('interesting' meaning perhaps 'safely re-
mote'), are inclined to label Li Po's 'imitations' as
merely escapist; but it was also a Taoist view to regard
the reality of imagination and of dreams as no less real
than what is usually called reality by contrast. The
Taoist philosopher Chuang Chou (latter fourth, early
third century B.C.) dreamt he was a butterfly; but when
he awoke said he did not *know* whether he had dreamt
he was a butterfly, or whether he was not now a
butterfly dreaming he was Chuang Chou.

Contemporary descriptions of Li Po speak of his
great, flashing eyes and loud, shrill voice. His presence
seems to have electrified everyone and the speed at
which he could compose, when in drink, to have as-
tonished them. He seems to have been the arch-poet as
envisaged by the romantic imagination, and in 'real
life'; so much so that his name has become much the
best known abroad of any Chinese poet, much like
Byron among English poets, to people who may not
have read any of his poems even in translation. But in
his own country and those that share its script and
culture, he has also been the most widely read of poets,
and must be one of the most widely read of all great
poets in the world's literature; and one of the most
influential, although he was no theorist and it is
very hard to say what exactly it is in his poetry that
captivates.

The well-known legend of his death, in 762, is that he
fell drunk from a boat while trying to grasp the reflec-
tion of the moon, and was drowned. It might even be
true, particularly as death from pneumonia seems to
have been described as 'drowning'. It is indeed always
difficult to separate fact and fiction about his life; a few
further details of which will emerge in the remarks on

his poems, though very little as a rule in the poems themselves.

4. Tu Fu

Tu Fu as a man is contrasted with Li Po in almost every conceivable way. His personality does not seem to have made any striking impression on his contemporaries, and there is no record at all of his physical appearance. Popular imaginary portraits of him sometimes represent him with an emaciated face, because of the hardships he underwent, a rather severe expression, and wearing some kind of official headgear. Some of these rather resemble some pictures of Dante, crudely copied from well-known portraits and cheaply printed. Such portraits seem to represent the Tu Fu of the old Chinese school-masters (whom they tend to caricature) and hardly invite one to read his works: Tu Fu has perhaps suffered even more from the praise of schoolmasters over the centuries than Li Po has from their blame. Other imaginary portraits which represent him as round-faced, bright-eyed and with an amused expression, holding book or writing brush, are both more attractive and more convincing. For all his indignation and his great suffering Tu Fu was a happy man in his basic nature, as in Confucian belief the good man must always be.

Although there have been many problems, such as the exact date of his birth which was only in recent times finally resolved, scholarship over the centuries has been able to compile a remarkably complete biography of Tu Fu, helped by his poems many of which refer to current events in the Empire and in his own personal life. The known dates of the former have often made possible the dating of the latter, and parts of the puzzle have gradually so fitted together that a great proportion of his poems (unlike those of Li Po) can now be dated and set in chronological order; adding much to their interest and meaning. Some of the latest of this research is set out in a very full biography of Tu Fu, illustrated with prose renderings of 374 of his poems, *Tu Fu: China's Greatest Poet*, by William Hung (Harvard University Press, 1952). There are some details of his life, too, in David Hawkes' *A Little Primer of Tu Fu* (Oxford, 1967), which gives thirty-five of Tu Fu's poems in the original with literal and prose translations, and with commentary. To both of these I am deeply indebted.

In the present book facts about Tu Fu's life, also about the age in which both poets lived, can best be given in the remarks attached to his poems; so only a little needs to be said about them now. Tu Fu was born in 712 at Shao-ling near the capital, Ch'ang-an (now Si-an Fu in the modern province of Shensi), of a family of the ruling class but not wealthy. Like Li Po, he displayed extraordinary talent in early youth; so that when he went to take the highest official examinations he was confidently expected to obtain one of the foremost places in the list of honours. To everybody's surprise, however, he was failed. It seems unlikely in view of his background that he lacked influence; and influence anyway, though it might affect a placing in the leading honours, would not make the difference between passing and failure. And he is known to have sought success assiduously according to the custom of his class and times.

Possibly some of his ideas may have been in advance of the examiners' (always a mistake!), but it may also be that he was over-confident and that his originality was less practical, in reply to the political and economic questions, than he supposed. Of his later career as an official, this at least is the judgement given in the official T'ang history; and it must be confessed that the equation of poetic with administrative talent was often less perfect in practice than in theory. But a suggestion made by William Hung seems to give the most probable reason for his failure: that he had been experimenting with prose styles and had evolved a very difficult one of his own at that time. Examples of this survive which are hard to construe and would have been quite unsuitable for official purposes. Later he took the examination again, but this time had every excuse for failure because an unscrupulous prime minister decided to judge the candidates himself and fail them all, in order to demonstrate to the Emperor that all possible talent for governing the Empire had already been selected.

Neither Tu Fu's failure, nor Li Po's omission to take the examination, completely ruled them out for official careers: there was also a 'special entry' for persons shown to be of outstanding talent in some way or another, which would mean in practice attracting the favourable attention of the Emperor himself or of some very highly placed person. Li Po was in this way appointed to a post in the Imperial Academy (Han Lin or 'Forest of Writing Brushes'), which was responsible among other things for drafting important state documents; and although he very quickly drank himself out of the job and, being seen as what would now be called a 'security risk', never got another, he is nevertheless piously referred to as 'Academician Li' on the title-pages of old editions of his Collected Poems* because it

*He is referred to as such on the title-page of the Sung dynasty printed 'variorum' edition of 1081; reproduced in photo-facsimile by Kyoto University Press and published with a concordance, which has been of great value in working on the translations here.

was unbearable for his admirers that he should lack some such civil service honour. Tu Fu, from a post he held last in his career, is similarly referred to as Tu Kung-pu, 'Ministry of Works Tu' even to this day (rather as if we spoke of 'Latin Secretary Milton'). The post was in reality only 'associate' and was probably little more than a sinecure to enable him to carry on with his real 'works', his poetry. However, the fact that it gave him a title in the public service remains important many centuries after his death.

Tu Fu himself hardly distinguished his poetic from his political ambitions. There was, of course, no notion of democracy or of political parties; so that any political activity such as political journalism, which would be a fair description of some of Tu Fu's poems, had to be within the one recognized political body, the bureaucracy. The distinction between this literary political activity and other kinds of political activity such as an advisory place at Court, which Tu Fu once briefly held, or a particular local responsibility in the structure of government, was therefore much less clear than it would seem to us. There was relatively little notion either of poetry being only 'artistic' and prose 'practical'. It was rather that while prose was suited to conveying certain kinds of facts and to shorter-term executive business, poetry (given a poet well qualified in all respects to produce it) might be much the more suitable medium for consideration of the Tao of government itself in relation to longer-term policy; or for informing the minds and spirits of policy-makers in less direct but still important ways; or simply as 'recreation' for them.

There were virtually no producers of poetry other than those at Court, or notionally at Court because they were members of the civil service (the only highly literate class), and there was no other public for it. Its function could therefore hardly be detached from the other functions of this ruling class which, of course, included the Emperors themselves, and among their number some great poets. There was no theatre at this time (T'ang), the 'spectacle' being dancing and mime; no novel and little other purely recreational prose (the respectable functions of prose being histories and essays). So the part played by poetry was very great indeed, and it was poetry more than anything else in literature that benefited from the new creative energy of the age. Tu Fu's ambitions for both a political and a poetic career, and the absence of a clear distinction in his mind between them, were therefore to be expected; and nobody would have ever thought him less a 'poet' for any of this. It is surprising to most foreigners now that Mao Tse-tung should be a highly regarded, though not prolific, *poet*; not merely a political leader who as a hobby produces verses.*

Had Tu Fu passed the examination and enjoyed a more prominent political career, he could still have been a very great and productive poet even if he had been prime minister. One of the greatest, most energetic and controversial of all Chinese prime ministers, Wang An-shih in the eleventh century, was famous also as a great poet, admired as such even by his many and bitter

*It would not surprise them at all if he were a great orator, which he is not. There was never a Chinese tradition of oratory, because it had no function in a despotism assisted by a bureaucracy; for there was never occasion to sway a large number of people, as there was no notion of majority decision. To influence civil service colleagues as individuals, poetry took the place of rhetoric; which is therefore a new thing to the Chinese in this century, and seems sometimes to have gone to their heads.

political enemies in his own day, and he is still given much space in every Chinese anthology. Nevertheless I think that Tu Fu's failure in the examination probably had one of the most beneficial influences on his poetry: as a warning against a tendency towards a too great density of meaning in his writings, and as a spur to his ambition for which poetry became the chief outlet.

A second great and beneficial influence, which he clearly acknowledged, was meeting Li Po in 744 or 745, with whom he stayed for a time. Tu Fu evidently did not disapprove at all of the motive of Li Po, who was already 43, in retiring from the world (that is from an official career). During his life Tu Fu wrote several poems to Li Po (significantly including dream poems) and Li Po rather fewer to him, as far as we know from what has survived. I do not think that any significance need be attached to this smaller number: Li Po, the older man, was less to be expected to write enthusiastic poems to the younger one. It might be, though this is of course speculation, that their striking complementary roles, which are unique in the history of Chinese poetry, were even somehow decided between them; that they themselves, in fact, invented 'Li-Tu'.

The third of the three most important events to influence Tu Fu's poetry was the tragedy for all China of the An Lu-shan Rebellion, a brief account of which will be given in an appropriate place (p. 171). This took place in 756, and all critics agree that from then until his death in 770 was the period of Tu Fu's greatest work. It is from this period that all but two of the poems in this small selection are taken.

The burden of 'greatness' which history has thrust on Tu Fu has been in some ways too heavy a one; at least for the enjoyment of his character and of his poems by so many who have had to 'do' him at school or by those who have otherwise been led to him in too great awe of his nobility, erudition and perfect versification. The real Tu Fu seems to have been one of the most human, approachable and attractive of great men who have ever lived. The language of many of his poems is now and always has been very difficult, because of the overlapping trains of thought (it has in fact a great deal to say!) and also because of a certain 'impedance' against a too-immediate understanding. Tu Fu understood the need for this, like other great artists. But once the difficulties, which are part of Tu Fu's art in particular, are broken through in his original language one is never left with anything heavy; rather with a strange and exciting lightness, even in those poems labelled his greatest and most serious. This is partly because his difficulties are always of an *intensive* rather than of an *extensive* kind: at first it is often difficult to see how words in some brief combination fit with each other or the thought can fit with the whole; but once this is done, one's own imagination takes over and one is no longer being *told* anything by the poet.

Most of Tu Fu's life was a hard struggle for existence. On more than one occasion his family reached a state of starvation, of which one of his children died; and his own health in later years suffered from his past privations. Almost all the ambitions of his youth seemed to be frustrated, and in the estimation of his day he was barely even in the first rank of poets.

All critics regard the highest Confucian virtue of 'compassion' as the outstanding quality in Tu Fu's character and poetry. But his honesty was perhaps his most exceptional characteristic of all. It allowed him to complain honestly when complaint he had, but never to sink into self-pity; to enjoy life to the full, when that was possible; but, sad or gay, neither to diminish nor to inflate his emotions or himself; always keeping a sense of balance, with which went also his sense of humour.

It is doubtful if Li Po, undeniably egotistical and his own hero (or sometimes 'anti-hero'), possessed this particular kind of humour. It was Tu Fu, extraordinarily devoid of egotism and instead an ardent worshipper of other heroes (including Li Po), who left self-portraits in his poems among the most perfect in the world: for the quality both of the portrayal and of the figure portrayed.

5. The Background to T'ang Poetry: The Beginnings: The 'Book of Odes', The Language and Script

In a work called something like 'Jottings from the Garden of Arts' by a sixteenth-century Chinese critic,* the outstanding qualities of Li Po's poetry are said to be *ch'i* and *tzu-jan*, and of Tu Fu's *yi* and *tu-tsao*; and many others have said the same thing in different ways. *Ch'i*

*Quoted in *Chinese Lyricism* by Burton Watson (University of Columbia Press, 1971). The critic's name was Wang Shih-chen. There is another important critic and theorist of poetry, who lived in the seventeenth and eighteenth centuries and who is quoted several times in another very valuable book on Chinese poetry, *The Art of Chinese Poetry* by James J. Y. Liu (Routledge & Kegan Paul, 1962), and whose name is also romanized as Wang Shih-chen though different in Chinese. This sort of thing can be very confusing, but the fact is that Chinese names romanized are not much more helpful than mere initials would be in another language. They are also extraordinarily unmemorable in this form (worse than Jones-Williams and Rees-Griffiths!) and so are on the whole avoided in this book. A rough guide to the pronunciation of romanizations is given on p. 11.

has the basic meaning of 'breath' but, like other words
in other languages with this basic meaning, it has ex-
tended meanings like 'spirit', 'psyche', 'atmosphere'.
Tzu-jan means 'nature', 'naturalness', 'spontaneity'
(including but not confined to the Nature of flowers
and trees and the weather: these, as much as words them-
selves, are a property of all Chinese poetry). *Yi* means
'mind', 'conscious thought'; and *tu-tsao* means 'making
independently', 'creativity'. Each pair of expressions
this critic chose suggests respectively the quality of the
Yin and of the Yang imagination, as described at
the beginning of this essay. They also suggest the
Greek contrast of 'Dionysian' with 'Apollonian' in the
arts.

Something must now be said about Chinese poetry
more generally, for neither of these poets was a world
unto himself. They had both forebears and posterity;
and despite the many contrasts between their characters
and poetry, they were friends because they had even
more in common.

The earliest recorded Chinese poetry is to be found in
the ancient anthology, according to legend compiled by
Confucius himself, called the *Shih Ching*, 'The Book of
Odes' or 'The Book of Songs' (translated under the
last name by Arthur Waley, George Allen & Unwin,
1937). This contains a little over 300 poems from per-
haps the twelfth century B.C. to about 600 B.C.; and
although these poems are mostly quite short (many of
them simple folksongs) and not 'epic', their place in
early Chinese education was similar to that of the
Homeric epics in Greek. The traditional arrangement
of this anthology is taken from an edition of the
second century B.C. by a scholar who belonged to a
'scholarly succession', like an 'apostolic succession', from

Confucius himself; who, even if he did not compile the anthology, attached great importance to it and frequently quoted from it. In this arrangement the first poem is called *Kuan Ch'ü*, from the first two main beats in the first line of the song, and is a Wedding Song probably from the earliest stratum in the anthology. The poem is traditionally ascribed to a marriage in the twelfth century B.C., which was of great importance to Chinese history; to say someone 'did not know his *Kuan Ch'ü*' was like saying he 'did not know his ABC'. Confucius refers twice to this song in the *Analects*: once for the 'joy without licence' of its words; once for a particularly pleasing choral performance, which 'filled his ears'.

A translation of this song follows, together with music originally transcribed in Chinese notation by the great Confucian scholar Chu Hsi of the twelfth century, but said by him to date in this form from the time of Li Po and Tu Fu. It is kindly provided, re-transcribed into our notation, by Dr Picken, and translated by me rather freely but equisyllabically and in its musical metre so that it can be sung in English. This metre, it will be noticed, is that of Longfellow's *Hiawatha* (copied by him from the old Finnish epic *Kalevala*); consisting of two pairs of trochees, *tumti tumti*, doubled to make eights: *tumti tumti / tumti tumti*; doubled again to make a stanza of sixteen syllables, and in the second stanza here one of thirty-two.

Apart from the contraction necessary for the equisyllabic translation into English (Chinese having, as David Hawkes puts it,* a different 'specific gravity'), it must

*In his essay 'Chinese Poetry and the English Reader' in *The Legacy of China*, edited by Raymond Dawson (Oxford University Press, 1964).

關 關 睢 鳩　　在 河 之 洲
Wa - ter - birds　on　Ri - ver　is - lands:

窈 窕 淑 女　君 子　好 逑
Shy　the Nymph our　Shep - herd's　cho - sen!

參 差 荇 菜　左 右　流 之
Wa - ter - li - lies Wreathe　a - round her:

窈 窕 淑 女　寤 寐　求 之
Shy　the　Nymph he　Wa - king,　slee - ping

求 之 不 得　寤 寐　思 服
Ne - ver rea - ches;　Wa - king,　slee - ping,

悠 哉 悠 哉　輾 轉　反 側
Long - ing, long - ing　Turn - ing, toss - ing!

參 差 荇 菜　左 右　采 之
Wa - ter - li - lies　To　a - dorn her:

窈 窕 淑 女　琴 瑟　友 之
Shy　the Nymph we　Greet with　zith - er!

參 差 荇 菜　左 右　芼 之
Wa - ter - li - lies　To　ar - ray　her:

窈 窕 淑 女　鐘 鼓　樂 之
To　the shy Nymph　Bell, drum bring glee!

be confessed that this translation differs from accepted interpretations since those of the Chinese scholars of the second century B.C., in that three verbs always taken as meaning gathering the waterlilies, supposedly to 'eat' *them* (making this a courtly version of a work-dance song), I have taken as meaning gathering them to 'adorn' *her*, the bride. She herself, described by a phrase meaning something like a 'maiden water-pure in the seclusion of grottoes' becomes in translation a 'nymph'; but hardly unfairly, especially as 'nymph' is also and originally the Greek for a 'bride', whose flowers all over the world where they grow are waterlilies, *Nymphaea* (more accurately botanically in this case, *Nymphoides peltata*, the Fringed Waterlily or Water Gentian).

The song was for the wedding of a prince, ancestor, according to the tradition, of the Great House of Chou; who ruled China from the twelfth to the third century B.C. The etymology of the word in Chinese used for a 'prince' in the song relates it to a 'flock of sheep' and so to a 'shepherd' (the etymologies of these words are reflected in the ideographs with which they are still written); and it does not therefore seem unfair, either, to retain this image in the translation to go with the 'nymph'. Some might object that all this makes the ancient Chinese song 'too Greek'; but how to make it 'Chinese', without making it simply *alien*?*

The birds in the first line were in fact ospreys, noted for their conjugal fidelity, 'Kuan-kuan!' being their cry; but most Chinese nowadays imagine them as

---

* A very distinguished scholar indeed has translated, without botanic justification, what is here 'waterlilies' as 'graded duckweed'. Is there a fear sometimes of bringing what is old and distant too close?

mandarin ducks, who are noted for the same virtue and have now taken their place as a symbol of it:

KUAN CH'Ü

Waterbirds on
River islands:
Shy the Nymph our
Shepherd's chosen!

Waterlilies
Wreathe around her:
Shy the Nymph he
Waking, sleeping
Never reaches;
Waking, sleeping,
Longing, longing,
Turning, tossing!

Waterlilies
To adorn her:
Shy the Nymph we
Greet with zither!

Waterlilies
To array her:
To the shy Nymph
Bell, drum bring glee!

The bride probably came by boat (as the tune seems to suggest, and as brides still often do in China), and the whole imagery of the song may remind the reader of English 'composed' poems in the Greek pastoral tradition, like Spenser's *Prothalamium* ('Sweete Temmes! runne softly, till I end my Song!') and Milton's *Comus*. There are, however, few later 'composed' poems in Chinese of this kind, and some reasons for this are worth looking into. In the first place, there was no need to imitate an old pastoral tradition; because there it was

49

ready to hand in this poem, which, although its uses of vocabulary and grammar are in fact archaic enough to cause great difficulties, is in what otherwise seems to be the Chinese language. It did not need remaking, as a Greek pastoral (in a line of descent perhaps through Latin, Provençal and French or Italian) might need remaking in English.

Three vitally important features of the Chinese language contribute to this apparent closeness in time and tradition. In the first place, Chinese is its own classical language with no conscious tradition of translation from other languages, at least not until a millennium and a half or more after this poem and then only directly or indirectly for the imported religion of Buddhism; in the second place, it has always been a language of words of one syllable not subject to the addition of grammatical endings, whilst its basic metres in poetry have always been *syllabic*. This second feature has the tremendous significance to Chinese literature and continuity of civilization that in modern pronunciation and regardless of widely differing dialects, all of which have this monosyllabic base, the most ancient poems retain the same basic metre and so still 'sound right' and please the ear. And in the third place, its system of writing has never been a phonetic one of analysing sounds separate from meanings and below the level of the syllable: that is to say, Chinese 'spells' syllable and meaning together, rather as we do with spellings like 'hare' and 'hair' for their different meanings; except that it has characters only for whole syllables and no tradition of analysis into a syllable's constituent vowels and consonants.

This third feature means that changes in the sounds of words, such as occur over the centuries in all languages, are disguised so that everybody naturally reads an ancient poem in modern pronunciation – even so ancient a poem as this. It is not merely that these most ancient poems are not in a language foreign to the Chinese, as Latin or Greek are to us, but they do not even look much different from the modern language in spelling or in the words they contain; to the extent that Chaucer or even Shakespeare in original spelling looks strange to us.

No Chinese language, in a literature of over 3,000 years, looks or has to be made to sound archaic in quite the same way as Chaucer does to us, though he wrote a mere 600 years ago:

> Whanne that Aprille with his shoures sote
> The droghte of Marche hath perced to the rote . . .

Words may sometimes change in meaning, perhaps gradually and hardly perceptibly but still significantly, as

> He was a verray parfit gentil knight

has changed to us. To understand this now we require a corrective supplied by scholarship. If I am right in my interpretation of *Kuan Ch'ü*, Chinese scholars of more than 2,000 years ago, but still many centuries after the song itself, who did not perceive that the three verbs for 'gathering' were also verbs of 'adorning' ('adorning *her*' instead of 'gathering *them*' makes better grammatical sense, too) froze the song in its usual modern interpretation. In this they were doubtless influenced by several songs of a 'Here we go gathering nuts in May' kind in the anthology; but also perhaps by a subconscious moral preference for the idea of a courtly version of a work-dance. (We may morally prefer our meaning of 'gentle' to Chaucer's!)

The Confucians did in fact considerably change the significance of many of these ancient songs by making them supposedly allegorical and giving them moral meanings in their own taste. (The Communists seem recently to have been doing something similar with other old poems.) The Confucian outlook could never adopt an 'art for art's sake' theory of poetry but always expected a poem to point some sort of moral, however inexplicit it might be, or at least somehow or other to make the reader wiser and better.* This became a generally accepted Chinese theory of all art, as much as the theory of the single Tao was applied to other things. It may even have had the very beneficial effect, opposite to what might be expected, of making Chinese poets and painters less rather than more inclined to point explicit morals; since those in the most ancient poems held up by the Confucians as examples were usually far from obvious!

It meant, too, that the slightest reminiscence in a later poem of an earlier one could make a sort of electrical connection to that poem's virtue; as if for us 'fisherman', for instance, carried a sort of *latent association* with St Peter, the degree of activation depending on the reader and context but always there. This is a reason for the great importance attached by the Chinese to 'literary allusion' in poetry; to which must be added the consideration of the vast literature, over many centuries, to which such allusion is possible because of continuity provided by the script.

There are other ways, too, in which Chinese is peculiarly suited to the development of this concept of *latent association*. But I believe that this concept is also one of great importance to the understanding of the nature of all human language; carrying as it does an

*I use the word 'reader' in its etymological sense of an 'understander' rather than as a reader only through the eye; which as already said was never done in early times.

assumption of free-will on the part of the reader to activate or not to activate such associations, guided by considerations *outside* the content of the communication-in-language itself. Recently there has developed in some places a strange structure of certain kinds of linguistics, pseudo-mechanistic and metaphysical, based on a *desire*, not always rational, to believe in the self-containment of the communication-in-language; largely for the needs of computing machines, but influencing all sorts of thinking. The tendency has always been there, however, in the West because of the traditional concentration of grammarians on the particular features of coupling apparatus, especially in our classical languages of Greek and Latin; but the Chinese, without such apparatus, were always more inclined to regard a communication-in-language less as the contents of a vessel than as the vessel itself, designed to *receive* meaning-in-context: hence the allusive rather than explicit nature of so much in the tradition of Chinese art, relative to our own tradition.

This does not mean, as is sometimes supposed, that the Chinese language is incapable of a 'precision' that our own languages possess. A language which has been the medium of government of the greatest empire in history, in terms of time and population, could hardly have such an inadequacy; and modern Chinese scientific writing is also often of the highest quality and a delight to read for its concise lucidity. The difference is that Chinese utterances have to be expanded in order to achieve certain kinds of precision which are built into our grammar in a way that gives us no choice. These are such things in Western languages as the distinction of the singular and plural of nouns (Chinese nouns, unless otherwise indicated, stand for the general concept alone); the compulsory use of subjects, including pronoun subjects, with verbs (Chinese verbs are autonomous and have no subject, except in the sense of what is being talked about *if* it is necessary to state that); present, past and future tenses, active and passive voices of verbs (less often necessary than we suppose, sometimes misleading, and also expressible by expansion in Chinese); and so on. Because of the in-building of these things into our grammar, our lawyers (who do indeed have to be precise) often have to expand their utterances greatly in order to *cancel* them, as in 'person or persons who are or have been or intend to be' and the like.

This difference is very important to the reader of Chinese poetry (though the apparatus of *our* language obscures it in translation) for Chinese poetry tends to be in the most concise and so most generalized form of the Chinese language; which is *not* the same as 'vague', but is such as to achieve vividness by giving greatest freedom to the reader's own imagination – in a scene that the poet himself has set. Something similar can also be observed in Chinese painting, which does not so much invite the viewer to take the artist's seat as to take his own walk in the landscape. (The translator of Chinese poetry has often to determine the walk more precisely than the original; but he cannot translate it into anything less than his own language requires.)

Chinese words are not themselves 'vague' either, though sometimes accused of being so by foreigners, but tend as a rule (because of the absence of grammatical clues) to distinguish meanings *more* carefully than we do. Yet, as might be expected of any language with so different a cultural ancestry from ours, a Chinese word may sometimes stand for a group of concepts that we have never thought of associating together, and which we cannot therefore cover with any word of our own: the associations we make being, much more than we realize, of common European and Near Eastern ancestry. Most often, however, even though we do not possess such a word, the associations latent in a Chinese word are not difficult for our minds (no different, after all, from Chinese minds) to grasp.

A principal source of the latent associations in the words of any language is to be found in their etymologies; that is to say, their histories. This need not mean, in English, knowing the Greek or Latin, Sanskrit or Gothic root to which, for example, a word like 'brood' is related; it may mean no more than an awareness of the *latent* association of the verb 'to brood' with a broody hen hatching eggs. People who are not especially interested in etymologies, however, will seldom think of the etymological significance of this 'brood' (which is also related to 'brew'); yet, if they use language attentively, they will keep alive the associations *as if* they were conscious of the etymology. Good observation of these associations in daily usage will make them cluster into a notion; that is, into a vessel able to *receive* all these associations.

The foundation of the Chinese system of writing, with characters each for a syllable and meaning together, is not so much 'pictographic' as it is often described, nor even 'ideographic', as *etymological*; and this fact has considerable importance to all the poetry that is written in this script, and to the Chinese attitude towards words generally. The etymologies represented in the characters, even though the Chinese are no more inclined than other people to think consciously about them, represent nodes or focal points for groups of associations; and not only are most of these groups of associations very readily understandable to us, but many of them are extraordinarily closely matched in our own language (and, of course, other languages).

Possibly human language, as we now know it and think of it, may not be of such far-reaching antiquity in the history of the human race as is commonly assumed; but rather the product, mainly, of a particular phase in that history such as, compared with its whole length, would be no more than a moment: the phase of a pastoral and simple agricultural economy, with a neolithic and bronze technology.* This at least is the world of the language of the Old Testament and of Homer (whose Greek vocabulary underlies so many of our modern scientific terms); of the roots of our native English words; and of the etymologies visible in the Chinese script. Pastoral metaphors, for instance, relating to the cultural state of this particular world, seem to have special force in all later language of religion and poetry: but they also underly every one of our thoughts.

The last English word in the translation above of *Kuan Ch'ü*, namely 'glee', represents a Chinese word written with the character †

樂

which stands for both of the meanings that 'glee' had in Old English: that is, 'joy' and 'music'. Some early

*It is an unpleasant thought that we might in a moment as brief, or even briefer, lose the faculty of human language as we have known it.

†Such a character may look at first sight complicated and slow to write. This form, however, is the equivalent of block capitals; and the character has only four 'letters' 白 木 幺 and 幺 like our G, L, E and E.

forms of this character (ranging from the earliest Chinese script yet found, which is of about the middle of the second millennium B.C.; and all before the first stabilization of 'spelling' in the third century B.C.) are as follows:

A tree (for a wooden sounding board) with strings.

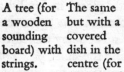

now written

is the tree.

The same but with a covered dish in the centre (for the idea of feasting).

Similar but with 火 for 'fire' replacing the tree. (For the idea of 'glow', which is also related to 'glee' in English).

As the first example, but with the addition of the sign for 'river'. (For the idea of 'flowing'.)

As the second, but formalized so that it is possible now to see the dish as a drum or gong and the strings as suspended bells, the tree as a stand.

As an exception to the general Chinese rule that a character represents the sound of a word of one syllable together with its meaning, this particular character not only represents both the meanings of 'glee' in English ('joy' and 'music') but differently pronounced syllables, in modern Chinese *le* and *yüeh*, for these two meanings respectively. The explanation of this anomaly is interesting, for it has been shown by the great Swedish sinologue Karlgren that each of these modern syllables once began with a sound like the 'gl-' of our own word 'glee'. There is, however, no need at all to suppose a surprising historical relationship between Old Chinese and Old English: the 'gl-' may have been felt as a gleeful sound by the speakers of both languages; while the Chinese at the time the character was created were conscious, even though the two words in their language were already not pronounced quite the same, of an *etymological* identity between them.

They were also aware of an etymological connection between these two words and their word for 'glow', just as there is between 'glee' and 'glow' in English; the word for this now being pronounced *shuo* but at the time probably with an initial like 'sgl-'. They therefore wrote it with the 'glee' character and the sign 火 for 'fire', to show the particular derivative of the etymon (root) they intended:

爍

A further derivative of this same etymon was the word for 'medicine'. We may not have a word related to 'glee' with this meaning, but we do make the same kind of association when we speak of a 'tonic'! The Chinese write their word with the 'glee' character under the sign for 'herbs':

藥 (The 艹 on top is from 屮屮.)

This is not the place to go further into the nature of the Chinese system of writing (which is not the anachronistic thing that too many Westerners take for granted that it must be, but suits the language for which it was designed perfectly); though a few more examples will be given with the next illustrative poem in this essay. The point I wish to make by the demonstration above is that the associations represented in these characters, like the nymph, shepherd and waterlilies as well as the music of the *Kuan Ch'ü* song itself, belong to a *universal language* of the human mind. Poetry working from such associations alone, without the other sort derived from 'literary allusions' to other poetry, or to historical events and the like, might be called 'primary poetry'; just as the tune to *Kuan Ch'ü* might be called 'primary music', in being immediately and universally comprehensible. (There is, of course, a need to distinguish the notion of 'primary' from that of 'primitive'.)

It must be expected that the poetry of such an age as that of the two poets of this book, an age of advanced material civilization with a history and literature that had grown for nearly 2,000 years from the time of this song, should be rich in 'secondary' features. Such features, insofar as they come from the local mythology, history and literature of China and are not universal, cannot of course be incorporated into the fabric of an English poem in the way they are incorporated into the fabric of the Chinese poem it aims to translate; and can only be supplied from the outside through the medium of notes. This consideration has naturally been a major one in determining the choice of poems in the present book, avoiding those so rich in 'secondary features' as to be heavily dependent on notes and therefore hardly capable of immediate impact on an English-speaking reader. But it is a fortunate thing that these two poets (like, I am inclined to think, the best poets at all times anywhere) never lost sight of the 'primary' in their poetry; and were usually able to give 'primary' force to 'secondary' features they incorporated.

6. The Background to T'ang Poetry: The Ch'u Tz'u

The $2 + 2 = 4, 4 + 4 = 8$ metre of *Kuan Ch'ü* was the
classic metre of the earliest Chinese poems; it survived
in poetry for more than 1,000 years and is still the metre
of proverbs and political slogans (like 'The – East – Is –
Red'). Such a metre could be enlivened by some syn-
tactic variation and variation in the degree, if not the
position, of the caesura but it became inevitably mono-
tonous (like the metre of Longfellow's *Hiawatha*) in
longer poems; even though all these poems were sung
or chanted in ways that presumably gave further oppor-
tunity for variation.

The Chinese name for regular syllabic verse of this
kind is *shih*; which, as it is the form of the earliest poems,
is also the word for poetry in general. The poems of the
next great ancient collection, the *Ch'u Tz'u** of the
fourth and third centuries B.C., are given the different
name of *tz'u*, which was to be used later for lyric poems
with lines of irregular syllabic length of the kind men-
tioned on p. 34.

The *Ch'u Tz'u*, of which the chief poet was Ch'ü
Yüan (*c.* 332–295 B.C.) who is the first named poet
of importance in Chinese literature and who wrote
its greatest long poem, the *Li Sao* or 'Encountering
Sorrow', consists of narrative poems and songs in a
quite different kind of versification from that of *Kuan
Ch'ü* and other poems in 'The Book of Songs'. Little
needs to be said about it here because it is not in the
direct line of evolution from the *shih*-forms of 'The
Book of Songs' to the *shih*-forms of T'ang times and

*Translated by David Hawkes, *Ch'u Tz'u: The Songs of the
South* (Oxford University Press, 1959).

of Li Po and Tu Fu; although it did greatly influence some of Li Po's poems in the freer metres, which quoted from and imitated the poems of the *Ch'u Tz'u* also in spirit.* Briefly, this form is characterized by the use of an interjection like a sigh (which is pronounced much like the word 'sigh' is spelt and was once pronounced in English). This was to mark the caesura in lines widely differing in length from four to twelve and more syllables. The 'sigh' interjection which occurs in every line of this poetry is nowadays pronounced *hsi*, so that this is sometimes called '*hsi*-poetry'; but although it has long been the custom to pronounce it every time it occurs, it may originally have been no more than an instruction to pause and perhaps strike harp or zither.

The spirit of the '*hsi*-poems' of Ch'ü Yüan and the other poets of the *Ch'u Tz'u* is one of ancient religious mysteries, airborne gods and goddesses, and rich symbolism (now mostly indecipherable) expressed in the names of flowers and trees. Some of these poems must be among the most flowery, in a literal sense, and botanical in the world; the varieties of flowers were particularized in a way quite alien to most T'ang poetry, in which only a few varieties – enough to give season and terrain – or simply 'pine-tree' or 'blossoming-tree' are ever mentioned because of the artistic philosophy of the times favouring simplicity and generalization.† In their

*A category of Chinese literature in more direct lineal descent from this anthology is the *fu*: a kind of effusion in unmetric but rhymed language. Though ours may not be rhymed, much of our own 'free verse' of today seems to me closer to the Chinese *fu* than to either *shih* or *tz'u*. This I think an inherent fault in attempts to translate Chinese metric verse into 'free verse' or prose.

†The T'ang poets were rather like the British Army which is said to recognize only three kinds of tree; 'pine-tree', 'poplar' and 'bushy-topped tree'. It is hoped to make the artistic reason for this clear below.

attitude to the mountainous Chinese landscape the poets of the *Ch'u Tz'u* are also quite different from the T'ang poets. They looked on it with brooding melancholy and fear as an uncouth place of frightening shapes, storms and wild beasts, comparable with the European dread of the Alps before the Romantic movement; not at all as the place of peace and freedom from the world that is found, for instance, in most of Li Po's poems. Nevertheless, Li Po also found the treatment of mountains by the *Ch'u Tz'u* poets exciting and imitated it in two of the most famous of his poems in this selection. Echoes from that anthology are found in all later poets: for example, the melancholy associated with the cries of monkeys and gibbons.

7. *The Background to T'ang Poetry: The Ballads and the Principles of Chinese Syllabic Metre*

In the *shih*-form of poetry, composition in the ancient four-syllable metre meanwhile continued until the first centuries after Christ, when two new forms appeared, probably from 'below'; that is to say, from the songs and dances of professional girls. These were to become not only respectable, but the chief classical metres of all later Chinese poetry; to which all the poems by Li Po and Tu Fu in this book are assigned in theory, and to which all but two (by Li Po) belong in fact. This may give the impression that Chinese prosody is dull and unadventurous; but these metres are no more than syllabic measures on which other prosodic features could be built, and it is hoped to show that as such they served their purpose excellently. They are the canvas rather than the painting.

The two new measures used the simple idea of a fixed but asymmetrical caesura. Instead of going $2 + 2 = 4$ like the ancient syllabic metre, one of them went $2 + 3 = 5$ and the other went $4 + 3 = 7$: both still very short lines by our standards or compared with some of the *Ch'u Tz'u* metres; and so suited to the kind of poetry – light but strong as steel, concise but vivid – that they helped to develop in succeeding centuries, culminating in the poetry of T'ang.

In all languages the pause has a meaning. In some, like Russian, it regularly serves where we should use the verb 'to be' between subject and predicate: 'A – B' meaning 'A *is* (a) B'. This is also a very common way of expressing the verb 'to be' as copula between subject and predicate in Chinese, especially in the concise language of verse; but I think that although this function of the pause may not be recognized in descriptions of English (or of Greek, Latin or French) grammar, because 'grammar' etymologically concerns the writing of languages and the pause is not notated except (in effect) in verse, *this meaning of the pause is never absent from any language*. If one says in English 'I go – home now', with a pause there, the meaning becomes 'My going (my journey) *is* home(ward) now'. In Chinese there would be no other way, because of the absence of the notion of coupling (like coupling waggons of a train) in their grammar, of distinguishing 'I go' from 'my journey'; or at least no other concise way such as would suit a poet. In all languages then, the pauses or timing of verse provide an extra kind of grammar; counterpointed with whatever other kind of structural grammar the language may possess in its prose. A fundamental rule of this extra kind of grammar (which is a universal and not merely local kind of grammar; not, I think, even confined to the human race!) is that what comes before the pause is a sort of subject and what comes after it is a sort of predicate.

Regarding the nature of the pause itself, I am most grateful to Dr Paul Kratochvil of the Faculty of Oriental Studies, Cambridge, for the following remark in informal discussion with him:

'Pause is one of the features within a larger pattern of prosodic features which act as signals in the segmentation of utterances. It does not necessarily have to occur in the physical sense of any particular articulatory gesture accompanied by a longer or shorter period of silence.'

Dr Kratochvil's use of the words 'signals' and 'gesture' (though, as he says, the latter does not have to be of any *particular* physical kind) seems to me important for the understanding of the nature of verse: that it uses the most ancient and universal of all languages, *gesture*, more than does prose. From gesture it is but a short way, if any way at all, to *dance*: perhaps the underlying melody of all verse, whatever forms of counterpointing its local language may make possible, is to be thought of as a syntactic dance? The *basic dance-measures* of the five-syllable and seven-syllable Chinese classic metres (in which it will be noticed that the second half-line for the 'predicate' remains the same length and in which I think that the fixed caesura will always come or seem to come centrally in *time*) then are respectively: *slow subject / quick predicate*, and *quick subject / slow predicate*.

8. A Demonstration by Ballad

The following ballad in the $4 + 3 = 7$-syllable metre,
which I have translated on the right in $7 + 4 = 11$-
syllable metre (needing this expansion for the different
'specific gravity' of English), is by the Emperor Liang
Wu-ti, who was born in A.D. 464 and reigned over the
south of a then-divided China from 501 to 549:*

Ho-chung-chih shui
  hsiang Tung liu,
Lo-yang nü-erh
  ming Mo-ch'ou:
	The waters in the rivers
	  all Eastward flow,
	At Loyang was a maiden
	  by name Mo-ch'ou:

Mo-ch'ou shih-san
  neng chih-i,
Shih-szu ts'ai sang
  Nan-mo-t'ou;
	Mo-ch'ou when she was thirteen
	  could weave and sew,
	At fourteen pick mulberry leaves
	  South on the row;

Shih-wu chia wei
  Lu-chia fu,
Shih-liu sheng erh
  tzu Ah Hou ...
	So at fifteen was wedded
	  to Mr Lou,
	At sixteen was child-bedded:
	  a boy, Ah Hou ...

Lu-chia lan shih
  kuei wei liang,
Chung yu yü-chin
  su-ho hsiang;
	The Lous have pavilions
	  with roofs so fair,
	Saffron and liquidambar
	  perfume the air;

T'ou-shang chin-ch-'ai
  shih-erh hang,
Tsu-hsia szu-li
  wu wen-chang:
	And she has twelve gold hairpins
	  put in her hair,
	For her feet brocade slippers
	  are hers to wear:

*The attribution is questioned but the song is not later than his
time.

Shan-hu kua ching	In coral hangs her mirror,
lan sheng kuang,	all gleaming, where
P'ing-t'ou nu-tzu	The caskets with these slippers
t'i li hsiang …	neat handmaids bear …
Jen-sheng fu-kuei	In a life of such splendour
ho suo wang?	what could be wrong?
Hen pu chia yü	She still would she'd been wed to
Tung chia Wang!	East neighbour Wang!

(see pp. 68–71)

It may be noticed that in the Chinese apparently the same syllable occurs with different meanings: *chia*, for instance, as a noun means 'family'; and as a verb (then having a different tone not marked here) means 'to marry'. Wang is a common surname like Smith to us. Lou, or more correctly Lu, is the name on the other hand of a notoriously rich family, which would have rung like Rothschild in sixth-century ears.

The name of the girl herself, Mo-ch'ou, probably originated as a strong negative expressing an affirmative, '*not* crying'; thus, a name like our 'Joy'. There are Greek and Indian names similarly formed (including that of the great Indian King Asoka, which is exactly equivalent to Mo-ch'ou); and there are some early Chinese names on the same model, for instance Mo-yeh, 'Undeflected', which is the name both of a famous lady and of a famous sword. But as a phrase in language, *mo ch'ou* was familiar as 'Do not grieve!' There was another Mo-ch'ou, in the T'ang dynasty, who gave her name to a kind of 'barbaric' music; but a T'ang work called 'On the Subjects of the Old Ballads' expressly says that her name, perhaps of a foreign girl and translated, had no connection with this ballad.

Nothing has yet been said here about rhyme in

Chinese verse, which has always had it from the earliest times. *Kuan Ch'ü* therefore rhymes, though I have not tried to rhyme the translation. Rhyming is considerably easier in Chinese than in most languages; despite the fact, important to the part it plays in verse, that it always has to be a root-rhyme because Chinese has no endings like '-ation' or like the rhymes of grammatical endings in Italian *terza rima*, to rhyme together. What is particularly easy to do in Chinese, compared with English, is to have long runs of the same rhyme: like the *-ou* in the first three verses here, with which *liu* and *fu* also rhymed, and the *-ang* throughout the remaining verses. In the translation I have been able to keep the first of these rhymes ('-ow' in English 'flow' sounding exactly like the Chinese rhyme) but I have not been able to sustain the *-ang* rhyme with my '-air', as the Chinese does, to the very end; and have to make a second 'change of key', which is the effect that a change of such sustained rhymes has in Chinese poetry.* Apart from the main rhymes, at the end of each line of the original (which I have written as the two half-lines, separately, with indentation after the caesura), there was an internal rhyme in the pronunciation of the time when the poem was written, between the syllables in the third verse† now pronounced *wei* and *erh*: then something like *gwié* and *nyié*.

This may help to show the extent to which Chinese

*The rhyming of this translation has, of course, been a matter of luck!

†I shall use the word 'verse' throughout this book for a printed quatrain which really stands for a Chinese couplet; and 'stanza' for a Chinese original quatrain or other division of a poem, that would justify this term. The structure of Chinese verse could be in stanzas from the earliest times; though it was usually written down as a continuous stream, the same as prose.

人 Man (*human male or female*)	珊 瑚 Coral	頭 Top ↑	盧 Lu
生 Live		上 On	家 Family
富 Rich	掛 Hang	金 Gold	蘭 Elegant
貴 Honoured,	鏡 Mirror,	釵 Pin,	室 Pavilions,
何 What	爛 Gleam	十 Ten	桂 Cassia wood
所 For which	生 Live (= gives birth to)	二 Two	為 Make into
望 To long?	光 Ray(s);	行 Line(s);	梁 Beam(s);
恨 Regret	平 Smooth	足 Foot ↑	中 Mid
不 Not	頭 Top	下 Under	有 Have
嫁 Wed	奴 Handmaid-	絲 Silk	鬱 Dense
與 Give(n)	子 -En (*child*)	履 Slipper,	金 Gold, (=*saffron*)
東 East	提 Carry	五 'Five'	蘇 Fresh
家 Family	履 Slipper	文 Figure	合 Harmony (= *liquidambar*)
王 Vang!	箱 Box!	章 Design;	香 Scent(s)

← Start here

十 Ten	莫 'Still (your)	河 River(s)
五 Five	愁 Grieving'	中 Mid
嫁 Wed	十 Ten	之 The
為 Make into	三 Three,	水 Water(s)
盧 Lu	能 Able	向 Towards
家 Family	織 Weave	東 East
婦 Wife;	綺 Fine silk;	流 Flow;
十 Ten	十 Ten	洛 Lo-
六 Six	四 Four	陽 -Yang
生 Live (= *gives birth to*)	采 Pick	女 Maid-
兒 Boy,	桑 Mulberry leaves,	兒 -En (*child; boy*)
字 Style(d)	南 South	名 Name(d)
阿 Ah (= *prefix of petname*)	陌 Row	莫 'Still (your)
侯 Hou! (= *Marquis*)	頭 Top;	愁 Grieving ('*Mo-ch'ou*')

See notes overleaf

The characters are to be read in columns, starting from the right, downwards (a vestige of the ancient custom of writing on a split bamboo held in the hand; the strips were then strung together, to read from the right). The first character 河 'river' has 氵 for ancient 川 meaning 'water'; which is now written 水 (and is the fourth character down) when used for the word 'water' itself and not just as part of another character.

中 'mid' (and 上 and 下 in the fifth column) follow their nouns. 之 is much changed from 㞢, depicting a foot, and meant 'that way': hence a general demonstrative and pronoun; also relating nouns to one another like 'de' in French. It can be seen eight times in the *Kuan Ch'ü*, sometimes in the last sense, sometimes for a pronoun object. 向 depicted a house with one window: a lighted window one went 'towards'? 東 is the rising 日, ⊙, sun behind a 木 tree; but earlier was ⊛, which was ⊛ a garden, but with a sign ↑ for roots: the East, where the sun comes from, as 'the roots of growth'. One picture often changed into another in this way. 流 'flow' is another such case: some see the part to the right of 氵 for water as a flowing 'tassel' ('bedeck, wreathe' is one of its meanings: see third line of the *Kuan Ch'ü*); others see 云 as 子, 㐌, a baby (sixth column): but *upside down*, being born, with 川 for the flow of waters at childbirth.

洛 is the name of a river, 'Lo'. 陽 is the 'Yang' of Yin and Yang; here for the north bank. The beta-like thing on the

70

left is a sign for a slope, incline and once was 㠯, a picture of stairs. The part on the right of it once showed men winnowing under 日, the sun. 女, 'a maid, virgin', was like 毋, 母, a kneeling 'mother'; but without the dots for the nipples. In the sixth column it occurs with 又, 又, 'hand', to make 'handmaid': the visual etymology in this character thus being the same as our own spoken word! The hand is seen also, tripled, in 桑 'mulberry leaves' (second column): many hands picking them from a tree. 兒, 𦥑, like 子, is for a diminutive syllable; on its own meaning 'child' or 'boy'. 名 'name' meant earlier 'fame', earlier still 'brightness, glory': it depicted the moon at a window, 口). 莫 depicted the setting sun; thence 'still(ness)' and a verb 'to still, cease'. In 愁, 'grieving, weeping', there is 心, 㣺, 'heart', with 秋, 'autumn';* the last being 禾, a tree with one leaf, and 火, 'fire'. (And so on.)

*'Grief' and 'autumn' sound rather similar in Chinese, also rhyme.

71

pronunciation has changed over the centuries since the ballad was composed. It has changed to a much greater extent still since 'The Book of Songs' and its *Kuan Ch'ü*; and neither that song nor this ballad would be comprehensible, or probably even recognizable as Chinese, in their original pronunciation to a Chinese now. As a result, many rhymes in older Chinese poems (including these of Li Po and Tu Fu) are obscured now; though the basic syllabic *metre*, as already emphasized, always remains unaltered. This particular gay and simple ballad would also be perfectly easy for the eye of any literate modern Chinese, and hardly difficult for his ear either to understand, read as it would be read now in modern pronunciation; but he might find it easier if he'd seen it first. (The old Emperor who wrote it, however, died some fifty years before St Augustine arrived at Canterbury.)

Ballads of this kind, from centuries before their own time, greatly delighted the T'ang poets, who, in this case, even invented something of a biography for this 'East neighbour Wang' and made him a poor scholar and poet like themselves, who died of a broken heart for Mo-ch'ou.

'South on the row' in the ballad is an allusion to another girl well known in song, Lo Fu, who (in a typical *pastourelle* of about the third century) was picking mulberry leaves 'south on the row' when a great lord saw her in her summer dress and with her white arms among the green leaves, and fell instantly in love with her. She tells him he has a wife already and she has a man, and anyway her silkworms are hungry so she must go. The reference to 'south on the row' therefore creates a situation, as a quotation like 'Nobody asked you, Sir, she said' could do in English; and one knows that Mo-ch'ou must have at least tried to refuse this rich husband. From 'In coral hangs her mirror ... neat handmaids...', following 'And she has twelve gold hairpins', one also knows that she looked at herself in the mirror ('Mirror, mirror on the wall') with her elaborate hair-do, saw the maid or maids come behind her with the grand slippers, and wished she were one of them ('neat', as will be seen from the literal translation, is 'smooth-topped'; that is, probably with straight hair parted in the middle and falling in neat plaits suitable to a domestic). Had she been, she could have married 'East neighbour Wang'.

Labouring such a poem is, of course, like explaining a joke (which is never then very funny) but it may be better to labour such points in this one than in the poems of Li Po and Tu Fu that follow. One of many things that both poets had in common, despite all the contrasts between them, was a great love of the old ballad literature and of the way it could so economically, without wasting a word, create first pictures and then, through the pictures, ideas. The discipline of writing in the short lines of the ballads, of five or seven syllables according to the syntactic dance-measure chosen, meant little room for description or rhetoric, and this assumed the reader's imaginative collaboration as expected by the old Emperor here; but of course that was to a much greater extent in poems of more profound thought than the story of Mo-ch'ou.

The greatness of T'ang poetry lies in the way the poets used the basic economics of these old ballads, sometimes imitating them closely in manner, sometimes using only their form for much more close-knit and complex poetic creation while still not losing the qualities of simplicity and lightness inherent in them, in order

73

to express whatever they wished to express, which sometimes had never been expressed in any kind of poetry before. The first thing to do, in their technique, was to take the reader out of himself and his trivial thoughts ('At once clearing the mind of common horses!', as Tu Fu says in one of the ballads in this book), not by exciting him with rhetoric but by making him immediately *see*, and so feel himself to be, somewhere else but where he was. The important thing was the immediacy of this vision; and for that the reader must be made unconsciously to reach out himself for it, instead of being told too much that he would have to accept and adjust to his own vision.

For this reason, the vocabulary of these poems tends to be more limited, probably, than that of any other great poetry in the world, because it prefers almost always the common word, which is also the general word, to the particular: 'winds' are almost always 'winds', much less often either 'tempests' or 'breezes'; brooks 'run' and seldom 'purl'; adjectives are sparingly used and then almost always as definitions rather than descriptions; and leaps in thought, for which the reader will not be too well prepared, are to be welcomed for renewing his vision; while at the same time a poem must be perfectly integrated, a thing made of one piece. Therefore simile is relatively little used and never extended, as it may be in our poetry, in such a way as to substitute a different image in the reader's mind from the main one of the poem. This, at least, was the general aesthetic of the age, accepted by both these poets, but it must not be expected that they themselves treated it as a set of rules and were not ready to depart from it in one way or another when the occasion seemed right. Li Po could write poems in a spirit of times before all this became the accepted aesthetic, and Tu Fu could write poems exploring beyond it: in some of which there is a good deal of poetic description of kinds more familiar to us; but both restrained by the aesthetic, and fresh because it was a new idea. (In later times, the T'ang aesthetic was often to become merely imitated and so exaggerated; too much was then asked of the reader, because the poems themselves were no longer an activity of exploration but simply dull.)

If the vocabulary was limited largely to the commonest words in the language, and constructions had to be simple because of the short syntactical spaces provided by the metres, this does not mean, however, that the poems were ever very easy.* The *vision* might be immediate, as was the aim; but, beyond the immediate vision and feeling of transference elsewhere (from where the reader was), the thought of the poem could be difficult to find because of what I have already called (speaking particularly of Tu Fu) the 'impedance' of the *tight construction*. This 'impedance', with its attendant ambiguities, is unfortunately, because it is an asset to the poems, something that belongs so much to the possibilities of Chinese grammar that I do not think that it can be reproduced in English. As a result, many of the poems here are a great deal simpler, one might say more facile, in some respects than the originals, hence denying the reader the stimulus of having a veil to break (what's a present without a parcel?) before getting to some idea. At the same time, of course, many of the ideas suggested

*In respect of the meaning of some lines in them, this would be a gross understatement. Native scholars (who do not always have the marked advantage over foreigners that the 'language lab' outlook on language supposes) often differ so widely in their interpretations that it would seem that one or other of these must be what, with any other language, would be called a 'howler'.

75

by the originals are simply not there at all in the translations. While a translator is only wasting his time if he adopts the defeatist attitude (which some think acknowledges no more than the truth) that great poetry cannot be translated, he must agree that the translation inevitably entails great losses; and endeavour to cut the losses by being prepared to accept some of them.

9. The Approach to Translation in this Book

The approach to the translation of the poems in this book is, to borrow a word used by Coleridge in his Notebooks, a 'poematic' one. Comparing a passage in Milton's *Comus* ('From her cabin'd loop-holes peep') with its source in a botanical description of the Indian fig-tree, he remarks:

If I wished to display the charm and *effect* of metre and the *art* of poetry, independent of the Thoughts and Images – the superiority, in short, of *poematic* over *prose* Composition, the poetry or no-poetry being the same in both, I question whether a more apt and convincing instance could be found, than in these exquisite lines of Milton's compared with the passage in Gerard, of which they are the organised version.

This notion of the 'poematic' as a sort of engineering term, rather than emotive word, for contrasting with prose (*the poetry or no-poetry being the same in both*) seems to me a useful one, worthy of revival if its users could be persuaded to keep it as such.

Both 'verse translations' and 'poetic translations' as names now carry off-flavours (which 'free verse' seems at present to escape, though *some* of that is not verse or 'poematically organized' at all). One distinguished

American scholar, introducing a book of German prose translations of the complete poems of Tu Fu, makes clear his feeling on the subject by contrasting them with those in 'poetic garb'. Yet, though one knows what he means, Tu Fu's own poems *were* in 'poetic garb' and were not, could never have been, made in prose. What is more, even the most painstaking and best prose translations of them give them very often different *meanings* from the originals; and themselves carry off-flavours, removing the poet from our sympathy by making him seem liable to being smug and a bore and full of both self-righteousness and self-pity (qualities from which it has confidently been stated above that he was extraordinarily free!), as a result of losing the *organization*, and so the timing and proportions, of what is said and of what is suggested in his poems.

Of course readers do not want to have such things *put* into 'poetic garb' for them at the cost of losing what the Chinese poet 'really said', but it is a fallacy to suppose that prose is not also a 'garb'; or that there is any way of knowing what the Chinese poet 'really said', short of learning Chinese and working with the battery of dictionaries, commentaries and concordances required for the job. (Few poems allow treatment like that given to 'The Waters in the Rivers' on p. 65; in which the 'literal renderings' are anyway selected as helpfully as possible.) The reader cannot, in short, ask the translator to do only half the job for him, so that he can do the rest: half-translation will only alienate any poet and freeze him for ever in an 'exotic' mould, when it would never have occurred to himself that he was 'exotic'!

It is fallacious, too, to think that because a translation has not been submitted to 'poematic' organization it must always be able to be at least more 'literal'. Often the very opposite is true, because the reader of a 'poematic composition' will welcome having to 'go out to meet it' (the phrase used by the great Confucian philosopher Mencius, 372–289 B.C.*) much more than he would welcome having to 'go out to meet' any piece of prose; while prose also has its *own* kind of organization, avoiding repetitions, rhymes and other kinds of echoes.

The belief in the superiority of prose for doing a more honest job of translating poems than verse is, of course, not without *some* good foundations. The following little Irish folksong was discovered by Miss Charlotte Brooke and published in her *Reliques of Irish Poetry*, 1789. It is given below with Kenneth Hurlstone Jackson's translation from his *Celtic Miscellany* (Routledge & Kegan Paul, 1951; Penguin Books, 1971).

Sí bláth geal na smér í	She's the white flower of the
is bláth deas na subhcraebh í	blackberry, she's the sweet
sí planda bf hearr méin mhaith	flower of the raspberry, she's
le hamharc asúl.	the best herb for beauty for
	the sight of the eyes.
Sí mo chuisle si mo rún í	She's my pulse, she's my
así bláth na nubhall cúmhra í	secret, she's the sweet flower
is samhradh ansan f huacht í	of the apple, she's summer in
eidir nodluig agus caisg.	the cold time between Christ-
	mas and Easter.

Miss Brooke had an intelligent, sensitive and profound appreciation of such songs, this one of which she alone rescued for posterity. Of it she wrote: 'The second of the two stanzas struck me, as being so particularly

*His book is translated by D. C. Lau (Penguin Books, 1970).

beautiful, that I was tempted to translate them both for its sake.' The second verse of her translation therefore will do:

> Pulse of my heart! – dear source of care,
> Stol'n sighs, and love-breath'd vows!
> Sweeter than when, through scented air,
> Gay bloom the apple boughs!
> With thee no days can winter seem,
> Nor frost, nor blast can chill;
> Thou the soft breeze, the cheering beam
> That keeps it summer still!

This, truth to tell, is much better and *less* boring verse, more faithful and *less* expanded, than most of the translations of Chinese poems that were made before Ezra Pound's *Cathay*, 1915, and Arthur Waley's *170 Chinese Poems*, 1918. These two revolutionized the business and produced translations that were not only poems in their own right, but found their way (against long-existing attitudes of English-speaking peoples towards translation) into general anthologies of English poetry. Pound's translations, as he had no direct knowledge of the language but worked 'from the notes of the late Ernest Fenollosa', were, as verse, guided only by his own excellent ear; and in their interpretations were sometimes very free or even haphazard, as in one deservedly famous poem, 'The River Song', which is wonderfully mysterious and beautiful in Pound's own style but consists of two quite different poems by Li Po run accidentally together with the title of the second incorporated in the midst of it!

The late Arthur Waley was, on the contrary, a most profound scholar of Chinese language and literature as well as one of the finest stylists in English prose in his lifetime. The theory of his method of translation, adopted since by most translators of Chinese verse into English, was to deal with the problem of the different 'specific gravities' of the languages by representing each word of the original with an English stressed syllable, then using unstressed syllables for the words he had to supply in order to make sense in English; with which, feeling able to use as many as he liked, he was very liberal. The success of his translations, especially perhaps of his favourite poet Po Chü-i and of the earliest collection of five-syllable poems, his *Seventeen Old Poems*, was outstanding and remains unequalled; but I think that his success was much more because of his great talent as a prose stylist than because of his theory. This, although he called it 'sprung rhythm' after Hopkins, did not use unstressed syllables like cats crouching before a spring but rather as a means of spilling away much of the energy in the Chinese lines; in the spirit of 'quietism' which was the special attraction of the Chinese mind to him, but very much in his own personal notion of it.

As for his prosodic theory itself, I think it placed much too much faith in the existence of a simple 'yes-no' contrast between stressed and unstressed syllables in English (surely a common failing in theories of English prosody, derived from classical Latin and Greek prosody in which there *is* a 'yes-no' contrast between long and short syllables?); while his liberal use of unstressed syllables, to come between the stressed ones which would not seem equally stressed if they fell together, sometimes greatly lengthened the short lines of the originals and led also to a somewhat 'Biblical style' as if an 'Exmoor pony' must always be called a 'pony of Exmoor' (like 'bull of Bashan'). Furthermore, having extended his lines in this way, which to me is weakening to their *visual* effect (a 'green coat' strikes my mental retina with much more force than a 'coat of green'), he often had to extend some of them, in order to match the others, by using words undeniably stressed according to his own theory but that did not represent anything in the Chinese.

This seems to have happened in the following translation, very beautiful as it is and with the grand phrase 'the shadows beat like wings'. That, however, is six syllables translating an onomatopoeic reduplicated syllable, *t'ung-t'ung*, in the original; which is one of a large class of visual and atmospheric adverbs in Chinese. Arthur Waley's translation represents a frequent use of it, but it can as often be used of such things as mountains looming out of mists:

In the last flicker of a dying lamp the shadows beat like wings;
Then it was I heard this news: you are banished to Kukiang!
I who was lying sick to death rose startled to my feet;
Through the cold window a dark blast blew the rain on my
face.*

In the original there is, in fact, neither 'feet' nor 'face'; which certainly could be nothing but stressed words in his theory, and which I think really have had to go in for the sake of the phrase ending with 'wings'.

Although very much disliking comparisons of translations of the same poem (*each* of which can only subtract from the effectiveness of the other, *both* losing conviction!) I give my translation of this poem, done before

*By Yüan Chen, written in A.D. 815 to the poet Po Chü-i on hearing of his political exile; from *The Life and Times of Po Chü-i*, by Arthur Waley (Allen & Unwin, 1949).

seeing Waley's – only because it will show the basic approach to translation in this book:

> A low lamp showed no flame
>   but looming shadow,
> Tonight came news of you
>   at Kiukiang, banished;
>
> Though ill and near to death,
>   I sat up startled:
> A dark wind blew in rain
>   through the cold window.

As in 'The Waters in the Rivers', I have put the Chinese half-lines on separate lines in this translation; but in some poems that follow, especially the longer ones (both representing the seven-syllable metre and representing the five-syllable one), I have written both half-lines on one line.

Here, however, and in almost all the other Chinese *seven-syllable* poems translated in this book, I have converted the $4 + 3 = 7$ syllabic metre into $6 + 5 = 11$ syllables (that is, adding two syllables to each half-line for the sake of the different 'specific gravities' of the languages*); instead of the $7 + 4 = 11$ metre which exaggerates the difference in length between the half-lines, producing a livelier dance measure that would not suit many poems as well as it perhaps does 'The Waters in the Rivers'. This $6 + 5$ syllabic metre in English, to which I have usually applied a further 'rule' of ending the first half-line with a *tum* and the second

---

*That it may not only be a matter of the 'specific gravities' of the languages, but that it may always be necessary for a translation to be somewhat longer in its lines than the original, is shown in translations of English poems into modern spoken Chinese by a poet of this century; in which he does something very similar: adding two syllables to each English line.

with a *tumti*, is the syllabic measure of the first quatrain of Bunyan's 'Who would true valour see, / let him come hither', now sung 'He who would valiant be / gainst all disaster'; and it seems to me a good basic measure in English, able to suit a wide range of poems by taking colour from the syntax and from the content in meaning, as does the original seven-syllable Chinese metre that it represents. The most literal English translation of the Chinese seems, therefore, often to fall into it: for instance, *an* (dark) *fêng* (wind) *ch'ui* (blow) *yü* (rain) / *ju* (enter) *han* (cold) *ch'uang* (window) becomes here 'A dark wind blew in rain / through the cold window'.

For the Chinese *five-syllable* metre I have done the same thing of adding two syllables to each half-line, thus turning it from $2 + 3 = 5$ into $4 + 5 = 9$ syllables; but without any general rule regarding stress, only local rules to suit some poems. The following is a little poem in this metre by Po Chü-i, the poet addressed in the poem above, who lived from 772 to 846:

> You've just said O!
> at your cold pillow
> When you notice
> light on the window:
>
> So deep the night,
> snow must be lying;
> Hark and again
> at bamboos breaking!

Both these very short poems are really quatrains (called by the Chinese *chüeh-chü*, of which something must be said in the next and final section, regarding tonal prosody), and the fourfold structure has something at once like a little sonata-form and like the composition of a painting. The sonata-form of these poems is reflected in the Chinese names for each of the lines (each pair of lines as printed here): the first is called 'Raising', that is, Introduction of the Theme; the second is called 'Forwarding', that is, Development; the third, 'Twisting', that is, Introducing a New Theme; and the fourth, Conclusion. Like painting, the beginning of such little poems usually represents in some way a background; while the end concentrates the senses on some often painfully sharp detail (the dark wind through the cold window and the crack of bamboo twigs breaking under the weight of snow); from which, as it were, they explode when the poem is finished into what students of Ch'an (Zen) Buddhism in the West call by its Japanese name of *satori*, Awareness.

It is in this way that it is possible for such a tiny poem (these have twenty-eight and twenty syllables respectively in the original) to be regarded by the Chinese (and by the Japanese, of course, also, in their even shorter *haiku*) as a great poem. But the possibilities of such a form are especially suited to the original language in which these poems are composed; as the great French scholar, Paul Demiéville, says in the Introduction to his *Anthologie de la poésie chinoise classique* (Éditions Gallimard, 1962):

A poem of twenty syllables could hardly be a great poem? But wait! Each of these syllables is a little world in itself, a linguistic cell irradiated with meanings like a faceted jewel. It throws out powerful resonances to both ear and eye, for it is written by means of a 'calligram', which is itself a work of art,* and its pronunciation has subtle modulations that play

* I am sure Professor Demiéville is right in stressing this as an integral part of a Chinese poem in the original; though many scholars and critics have reacted against what they have felt to be the excessive attention, also rather wrongly based, it has been given by some.

their part in the prosody. Thus it can touch aesthetic sensibilities in centres of the mind hereditarily given such exercise, for which our psychology and our physiology seem scarcely to have any equivalent.

With regard to rhyme in the translations in this book, I have used such rhymes as between 'shadow' and 'window' and between 'pillow' and 'window' in these two poems, when they meant no deviation from the meaning; also some rhymes off the beat, like 'O!' and 'pillow', as in the Irish classical *deibhidhe* metre. But I have nowhere (except in 'And so now spring ends' and 'The Waters in the Rivers') tried to follow an original Chinese rhyming scheme, and have only let rhymes come as they come. This has sometimes allowed the rhyming of a whole poem, but more often I have used occasional rhyme or half-rhyme as here.

Rhyme seems to me to have two distinct functions (though nobody need distinguish them to enjoy it): one as an integrator of a poem, giving it authority and making it memorable; the other for making a kind of pun. Regarding this latter, a pair of words will sometimes be found to rhyme both in English and in Chinese because both languages permit the same kind of 'punning rhyme'. A case in point is 'cloud' and 'crowd' in English, related respectively to 'clod' and 'curd', and both representing the idea of a conglomeration; which replaced older words for their meanings that did not rhyme. In Chinese 'cloud' and 'crowd' are *yün* and *ch'ün* which are variants, from a prehistoric time when Chinese had grammatical and word-forming inflections affecting mainly the beginnings of words, of a single root which has this same meaning of a conglomeration. (As the Chinese script is essentially *etymological*, such rhymes are often *visible* in it.) Other such cases could be cited, such as 'nest', 'rest' and 'west', 'mist' and 'dust', which work as 'punning rhymes' in both languages. These, like 'cloud' and 'crowd', are not always accidental in origin; but even where they are, they still contribute to poetry. Therefore, although it may be questionable whether occasional and unschematic rhyme has much good precedent in English verse, it seems to me a sound 'poematic' feature when available to a translator trying to get near to the spirit of the original.

As for the syllabic frames of these translations, it must be confessed that they do, of course, affect the choice of words in English (although, as already remarked, a prose 'frame' would do the same).

In particular, they sometimes cause a colourful detail simply to be left out. For example, a sentence that in good prose translation is translated as 'I remember a year or so ago, where the road wound east round my Brocade River pavilion' becomes in my translation only 'I recall near my hut / on Brocade River' – eleven instead of twenty-four syllables. The original, however, such is the difference in 'specific gravity' of the languages, has said all that the prose translation says in only *seven* syllables! Bearing in mind that sacrifices there must be in any kind of translation, I do not believe that such losses are always grave; while sometimes I think they may hardly mean a loss at all. Though great poets such as these never put anything in their poems only for the sake of metre and rhyme, metre and rhyme always make up part of the score and it would be an impossibly idealized view of the business of making poetry that supposed it did not.

Another way in which the metre affects the choice of words in the translation is in the use of such an anachronism as 'glass' for both '(polished bronze) mirror' and 'wine-cup' (which would be of lacquer or pottery); but I am inclined to think that, without self-conscious modernization like 'Shakespeare in modern dress', such anachronisms are better in any kind of 'poematic' translation than the suggestion of an antique shop. More serious but unavoidable are such things as the relatively colourless 'bough' instead of 'willow-bough' on the bank of a river, and 'great rocks' where the Chinese has a less common and much grander word than 'great' but still only of one syllable; or where, it must be said exceptionally, rhyme has been allowed to play a part in making 'pink as a peach's flower' become 'pink as a peach's skin'. ('Peach' in these poems always refers to the Chinese wild flowering peach-tree, ancestor through Persia of all our peaches, and never that I know to the fruit.) Some of these changes are serious and regretted as such, but I do not think that further confessions either here or in the notes to the poems can really do much to repair them, or to bring the reader closer in feeling to the originals.

Some Chinese words and expressions have no equivalent in our language at all: the reduplicated onomatopoeic adverbs like *t'ung-t'ung* above, for example. Other words have acquired associations which are in effect their meanings alone in many contexts; like 'golden', as in 'In Good King Charles's golden days'. Such a word is 'jade' (used more than 'gold' in these senses in Chinese): a 'jade flute' means no more than a flute of 'golden' purity of tone. Elsewhere, 'jade stairs' means 'marble stairs'; to keep 'jade' in such places would seem to me 'half-translation'. (The translation has always to be 'to taste', and in some places I keep the 'jade'.)

Less grand than 'jade' is what I have translated as 'jasper'. This is really a colour-name that can be 'green' or 'blue' or 'grey', but always has an association with *stone*. Chinese colour-names are quite different in concept from ours, for the whole matter of naming colours is more arbitrary and conventional than we commonly suppose. (Colour-names in Ancient Greek present similar difficulties.) The Chinese have a word for a *growing green*, which can also be used for the blue of the sky under which things grow and for the black of rain-filled clouds; and another for a *stone green* (or blue or grey) which is the one I have translated as 'jasper'. It is interesting that these words respectively match very well the Gaelic *gorm* and *glas*; so that the definitions in Dineen's *Irish Dictionary* and in Mathews' *Chinese Dictionary* are almost identical.

We start painting, mixing blue and yellow to make green, at Kindergarten, and so think in pigment colours; but, as anyone who has had anything to do with theatre lighting knows, the rules for spectral colours are quite different. It seems also that texture and other associations may be felt as integral with colour.

Lastly, there is the matter of numbers: Chinese constantly speaks of a hundred or a thousand or ten thousand (a 'myriad') where we should use only a plural, a distinction Chinese grammar lacks, or 'many'. Sometimes in poetry, too, less rounded numbers are used ('48,000' seems to be a favourite of Li Po's). Some of these exaggerations I keep, but some would be merely distracting to members of a more numerate society than that of T'ang.

10. The Tones and the 'Chinese Sonnet'

In the reign of the Emperor Liang Wu-ti, poet of 'The Waters in the Rivers', a scholar and prosodic theorist named Shen Yüeh (A.D. 441–513) investigated the four intrinsic tones in the words of the Chinese language of his day. Such tones, which although they have undergone various alterations are still a feature of all Chinese dialects, he named 'Even', 'Rising', 'Departing' and 'Entering'. (The story goes that the Emperor Liang Wu-ti asked him rather sceptically what they were, to which he dutifully answered: 'As Your Majesty pleases', using the four tones in succession.) From the point of view of prosody, he divided these tones into two classes: 'Even' and the rest, which he called 'Slanted'; and he proposed that for euphony in verse the two classes should be patterned and set in contrast one with another.

The best way of explaining the nature of these tones in Chinese to an English speaker may be to contrast English words like 'úndó' and 'thírtéen', which can be evenly stressed on both syllables (even if they are not always so, but can also be more stressed on either of them), with words like 'cóntrast' and 'contrást'; the latter having a different stress according to whether it is a noun or a verb; or with any other words of unequal stress ('Mónday', 'todáy') in our language. 'Úndó' and so on would then be 'Even'; while the rest would be 'Slanted'. These English examples, however, are all of words of two syllables (and 'Even' ones are also rather rare); whereas the similar distinction in Chinese applies to words of one syllable, and the quality of the distinction is also not quite the same. In modern Chinese ('Mandarin' dialect of Peking) there are now four tones, not the same as those of Shen Yüeh which are more perfectly kept in Cantonese as spoken in Hong Kong: the Pekinese tones being 'High Even', 'Low Even', 'Rising' and 'Departing', with no longer an 'Entering Tone'. These, to give an idea of the nature of the tones, are respectively something like: 'one' in 'one', 'two', 'three', tensely (that is firmly) counted without other expression; 'one?', also said firmly because fully expecting the answer 'yes'; 'one?!', with a touch of incredulity, and so not firmly; and 'one!', with an air of resignation and so also not firmly. But in Chinese these distinctions of tone are not a matter of expression (which is done in other ways, just as French says 'moi, je suis . . .' instead of 'I am . . .'). They distinguish different words as much as we distinguish, say, 'dog' and 'dig' by giving them different vowels.

Musically these tones differ greatly from dialect to dialect (for instance in Cantonese the 'Even' tone tends to fall musically at the end, whereas in Pekinese it is level; while the 'Departing' tone in Cantonese is musically level, though dying in energy, but in Pekinese falls in pitch as well). The prosodic distinction between the two tone classes is, however, maintained; the 'Even' tone-class (which includes both the 'firm', first two tones of Pekinese) is relatively *tense*; while the remaining tones are relatively *slack*. Some combinations of tense and slack have a more agreeable effect on the ear than others; and variety and contrast in this matter are particularly enlivening, whereas some kinds of repetition are deadening in effect. Shen Yüeh and poets after him therefore evolved rules in order to avoid such disagreeable effects. These rules, as might be expected, were mainly negative (one must not do so-and-so) and he listed 'Eight Faults' which, as it happens, are similar in some of their names to 'Eight Faults' in the sister art of calligraphy: such as 'bee's waist', too weak between too strong; and 'stork's knee', too strong between too weak.

An outcome of all this was a new kind of verse, still today called 'Modern Verse' in contrast with the tonally free 'Old Verse'.* This new kind is also appropriately called 'Patterned Verse' (more usually translated as 'Regulated Verse', which is literal but not perhaps quite so expressive of the idea). In it the tones might be patterned, for instance in a $2 + 3 = 5$ syllable line as 'slack slack / tense tense slack', rather like the idea of the foxtrot's 'slow slow / quick quick slow', but in terms of tension instead of time; and in the next line followed by a reversal of this rhythm into 'tense tense / slack slack tense'. (An example of such a five-syllable, patterned poem in its original pronunciation and with the tone classes marked will be found on p. 177.) The tonal metre is not like the foxtrot's *time*, because the Chinese syllables are all at least theoretically equal in length. Even though some maintain that this is not so in fact, but that the tense syllables are slightly longer than the slack (just as 'thirteen' may be slightly longer than 'today') neither this rather doubtful and unstable matter of length nor the matter of difference in pitch between the tones is the key to their place in the new patterned prosody as much as the difference felt in *tension*. It was this that made it possible to have a counterpointing prosody with a clear 'yes-no' distinction, like that of long and short syllables in Greek and Latin, to orchestrate with the basic melody of syntax and meaning, in the frame of the syllable-count which, of course, serves for the *time*.

The effect of this orchestration cannot, of course, be reproduced in English at all, belonging as it does to the phonetics of the Chinese language; but the age that

*It is hoped that the reader will resist the Western temptation to moralize about the 'stagnation' of Chinese civilization! Other *more* 'modern' kinds of verse did follow; though these two kinds did not die, and this expression for the difference between them remained convenient.

introduced it was an age with a passion for patterns and it introduced as well a kind of *semantic* patterning to the new verse forms. Of these the chief was a poem of eight lines in the five-syllable or seven-syllable metres (and so sixteen half-lines, either $2 + 3$ or $4 + 3$; the underlying syllabic metres remaining unchanged). In this the semantic patterning made it mandatory for the third and fourth line and for the fifth and sixth line to form couplets with 'rhyming sense' word for word. For instance, where one line of such a couplet had 'high', the other must have a word felt to be in the same adjectival class, like 'low' or 'great' or 'swift'; where the first had 'mountain', the other might have 'sea' or 'river'; and there must be similar correspondence, usually called 'verbal parallelism' or sometimes 'antithesis', in verbs and adverbs; and so in the whole syntax of the lines. (Inscriptions hanging in Chinese restaurants consist very commonly of auspicious couplets of this kind.)

Such 'rhyming sense' or 'verbal parallelism' is, of course, a common device in all the world's poetry. A good example, cited in Hawkes' *Chinese Poetry and the English Reader*, already quoted from, is:

> And bonny sang the mavis
> Out o' the thorny brake;
> But sairer grat the nourice
> When she was tied to the stake.

In less simple and longer English lines, however, the idea may be kept but not so word-for-word; as in

> Where doves in flocks the leafless trees o'ershade,
> And lonely woodcocks haunt the wat'ry glade
> (POPE 'Windsor Forest')

this in Chinese five-syllable verse might be something like

Flock(ing) dove / cover   bare   tree
    ↕   ↕   ↕   ↕   ↕
Lonely woodcock / haunt water(y) space.*

Here each word is expressed in Chinese by one syllable: the word-for-word parallelism is scarcely even avoidable because of the dependence on word-order and prosodic pauses in the grammar of a language that does not use grammatical couplings. Like rhyming in sound, this device is therefore much easier in Chinese than in English; and so is less artificial in effect than its strict observance in mandatory positions within a poem would be in our language. Nevertheless, it *is* often very artificial in the verses of some Chinese poets, who do not so much employ as make themselves the employees of the rule, which greater poets (including Li Po, and Tu Fu who is the acknowledged master of all time of the form) do not always even observe at all.

This eight-line form, having the tonal patterning and the mandatory central couplets with verbal parallelism, will be called here the Chinese *sonnet*; an analogy also made by David Hawkes, and I think a most appropriate one for the part it plays in Chinese poetry.† The follow-

*The Chinese do not like the lines of such couplets so much to rhyme as to contrast musically with one another.

†*Chüeh-chü*, as in the preceding section, were commonly written in the tonally patterned verse, often also with verbal parallelism in either or both couplets. Theoretically they therefore came to be regarded as 'sonnets cut short', which is what the name *chüeh-chü* means; but similar verses, of which the conception is much older, were also written in tonally free 'Old Verse'. (The old and new kinds are indistinguishable in translation.)

93

ing, to illustrate the form, are two sonnets, respectively in the five-syllable and seven-syllable metres and both Buddhist in inspiration; the first by the great painter Wang Wei, 701–59, who is regarded as the father of Chinese landscape painting and who as a poet stands beside Li Po and Tu Fu in the eighth century's golden age:

ON GOING BY THE SHRINE OF STORED INCENSE

> Where does it lie,
> Shrine of Stored Incense,
> How many miles
> into cloudy peaks?
>
> Where ancient woods
> have no tracks of men
> Deep in mountains
> sounds somewhere a bell;
>
> Waterfall's voice
> coming from steep crags
> And sun's colour
> cold on the larches,
>
> A pale stillness
> erasing lake's rim,
> Meditation
> tames Deadly Dragon!*

The second verse of this, representing the first of the two mandatorily parallel couplets, is word-for-word in the original language something like

> Ancient wood / without man track
> ↕   ↕   ↕   ↕   ↕
> Deep mountain / what place bell.

*The Deadly Dragon (the supposed monster in the lake) is the Passions.

One might wonder whether 'without' and 'what' are really good parallels to put in a class with the others; but in Chinese verse parallels too perfect would be, and alas sometimes are, just as boring as they would be in English. This art of verbal parallelism, counterpointed with the sound of the verse, provides the Chinese with some of their deepest pleasure from poetry when it is well done.

There is only one rhyme ever in a Chinese sonnet: here XAXA, XAXA ('peaks', 'bell', 'larches', 'Dragon'). But very often the first line also rhymes: AAXA, XAXA. The rhyme-scheme of the first half of such a sonnet, which is also very commonly used for a whole *chüeh-chü*, is then like that of each stanza of Edward Fitzgerald's translation of *The Rubáíyát of Omar Khayyám*.

The second example is by Li Shang-yin, 813–58, of whom several poems including this one are translated by A. C. Graham in *Poems of the Late T'ang.**

WRITTEN ON A MONASTERY WALL

To leave life, seek the Way,
    follow the others,
Which asks much, begs the brain,
    hollows the body;

Great gone, to see the World
    a grain of millet,
Small comes, to make it fit
    the Mystic Pinpoint:

Oysters, their wombs unfilled,
    long for the full moon,
And amber until made
    sighs for its past pine;

*Penguin Classics, 1965.

But faith in Holy Writ
for the true message
Hears Present, Future, Past
all in one gongstroke!

In translating this, I have brought into the text a Buddhist saying referred to in the original only by allusion: 'To see the World (in) a grain of millet'; which is very like William Blake's 'To see a World in a grain of sand', the first line of *The Auguries of Innocence*. It happens that there are two other of Blake's beginnings of poems in this quite short Chinese poem of nearly a millennium before his day: 'Hear the Voice of the Bard, / Who Present, Past and Future sees'; and, inevitably disguised in translation, 'Tyger, tyger, burning bright': 'Tiger-bright' being the literal translation of the Chinese for 'amber'. These are 'literary allusions' that a literary-allusion hunter would certainly find, if there were any possibility of their being such; and undoubtedly he would make much of them, with three in so short a space. But the human mind also shares allusions, the allusions most important in poetry: another of which here is, of course, the 'Mystic Pinpoint', shared with medieval Christian mystics.

The Chinese sonnet, of which six examples by its greatest master, Tu Fu, will be found among the poems that follow, is still alive as a verse-form today; and it may be appropriate as a reminder of the continuity of Chinese poetry, and also because it affords a good example of the role of literary allusion in it, to end this Introduction with a sonnet by Mao Tse-tung (born 1893) celebrating the eradication of the scourge of the water-borne parasitic disease, schistosomiasis, from a region in the Yangtse valley that had been notorious for it. This poem is the second* of a pair of sonnets composed on the occasion (as emperor or high official might have composed them at any time since the sonnet was invented); with a prose preface, like one preceding a poem of Tu Fu's among those that follow.

FAREWELL TO THE GOD OF PLAGUES

1st July, 1958

I had read in the issue of 30th June of *The People's Daily News* that in Yüchiang District they had exterminated the blood-sucking parasite. One after another, floating thoughts were wafted through my mind, so that when night came I was unable to sleep. But when a light breeze, sweeping in warmth, and the rising sun approached my window, out into the distance I gazed at the southern skies; and, joyously, I took command of my brush!

> Spring winds move willow wands
> in tens of millions:
> Six hundred million we
> shall all be Sage-Kings!
>
> Our red rain to the mind
> translates as torrents,
> Green hilltops are at will
> turned into bridges:
>
> So, silver spades, sink sky-
> scraping Five Ranges,
> And, iron arms, sway earth-
> quaking Three Rivers:
>
> Tell us please, Prince of Plagues,
> your choice of journey?
> Candles and paper boats
> blaze the skies for you!

*The first of the pair is a night poem and a dream poem, with mythological allusions making it more difficult to translate.

In this the 'Sage-Kings' translates the names Yao and Shun, rulers of China in a mythical golden age of pre-history beloved of the Confucians and placed in the third millennium B.C.; but no more of a literary allusion to any Chinese reading it than if these were, say, Abraham and Isaac from the Old Testament in our literature. The 'Five Ranges' are the great barriers to communication in China, and the 'Three Rivers' are the Yellow River and its tributaries the Lo (already met with here, in 'The Waters in the Rivers') and the Huai: rivers notorious throughout Chinese history for their disastrous flooding; and now, since the year before this poem was written, the subject of a vast engineering scheme for their control. 'Candles and paper boats' refer to traditional funeral ceremonies. Nobody in the poem's native land could have difficulty with any of these references, or fail to know of the God of Plagues or Prince of Plagues himself.

There is, however, something more like what is generally meant by a literary allusion in Chinese poetry, of the kind that if missed takes a lot of the meaning from the poem, in 'red rain'. This is a great gathering point of associations, such as is much loved in Chinese poetry, which, as has been said, always aims at *intension* rather than *extension*. In the first place, there is the obvious political meaning of 'red', with 'rain' for fertility and productivity. But 'red rain' is also a quotation from the great ninth-century poet Li Ho (whose reputation has recently much grown, and a number of whose poems are translated in *Poems of the Late T'ang* referred to on p. 95). In Li Ho's poem it means 'falling peach-blossom' but this, too, is a symbol with an ancestry in Chinese poetry, going back to a story by one of the greatest of all Chinese poets, T'ao Ch'ien or T'ao Yüan-

98

ming, A.D. 365–427; from which story it has meanings such as 'imagination' generally, and 'imagination of a Utopia' particularly. This Utopia is one of the simple life and of love of nature; so that, with the 'verbal parallelism' setting it against 'green hilltops' in the lines, there is an indication of the Chinese genius in art and a suggestion that the same energy and imagination may be turned towards the national needs for science and technology. The derivation of all these suggestions from this phrase and this verse is fully in the Chinese poetic tradition.

T'ao Yüan-ming's story is a very simple one,* with its like in fairytales all over the world, of a fisherman who followed a stream until he came to a grove of blossoming peach-trees on either bank. Exploring further, he came to a cave. Disembarking he climbed through and soon came to the light of day, where he saw a happy land, like a garden with its mulberry trees and willows; and when he spoke to the people, he found that they knew nothing of all the evils that had befallen the world in the last five hundred years. They entertained him graciously until he felt that he must return briefly to the world he had left, but they told him to say nothing of where he had been. On his way home he left marks so that he should have no difficulty in finding his way again, but once back he told of his wonderful adventure. Then, accompanied by officials, he led the way back; but, as the reader will expect, found no marks and no cave. Logically, one might therefore say that the story is of a mere illusion; but this has never been its meaning in Chinese literature. More than one of the poems that follow, by both Li Po and

* A translation by Cyril Birch will be found in *An Anthology of Chinese Literature* (Penguin Classics, 1967).

Tu Fu, refer directly to it; whilst neither the fisherman, who will be mentioned in another quite different context but still as the artist, nor the peach-blossoms are ever without *latent* association with it.

The well-informed reader of current affairs may at this point say 'Yes but . . .', refer to the Cultural Revolution, and suspect that all this is sinophile sentimentality. If it is sentimental, then it is false (the Chinese have never been a particularly sentimental people); and as for the Cultural Revolution, that is beyond the scope of this book, which is certainly not a political one. I only dare to suggest that it is important to know something about the imagination of a people, as can be seen nowhere better than in its poetry, even for understanding such a thing as the Cultural Revolution; though understanding does not invariably mean approval! And that without such knowledge, which can be obtained also from many much better books than this, some of which have been referred to in this Introduction, one may believe in much greater and far more dangerous fictions than the Story of the Peach-blossom Cave.

As Walter de la Mare says in the Introduction to his anthology, *Love*:

Minute narratives are implied, as it were, in some of the ancient Chinese poems, yet their characters, remote though they are from us in time and space, might, if this is not an immodest statement, be ourselves.

*

11. *Reading the Poems in English*

The translations that follow are intended to be read aloud, as were the original Chinese poems. For this, the caesura should always be given attention as a 'signal', even though (to quote Dr Kratochvil again) 'not necessarily as any particular articulatory gesture or period of silence'.

In both the regular classical metres, translated here respectively as 9 and 11 syllables, the asymmetrical caesura comes 5 syllables before the end of the line; and so comes after the first four syllables of the 9-syllable lines and after the first 6 syllables of the 11-syllable lines:

> There we heard owls hoot from mulberry leaves,
> Saw fieldmice sit upright by their holes,
> At deep of night crossed a battlefield,
> The chill moonlight shining on white bones,

and

> Since our T'ang times began, in painting horses
> We counted but one Prince inspired divinely.

In some poems I have thought it easier on the eye to leave the caesura unindicated; but in others I have divided the line in two at the caesura, indenting the shorter part:

> Where the dogs bark
> by roaring waters

and

> In front of K'ung-ming Shrine
> stands an old cypress.

LI PO

ON VISITING A TAOIST MASTER
IN THE TAI-T'IEN MOUNTAINS AND
NOT FINDING HIM

Where the dogs bark
by roaring waters,
   Whose spray darkens
the petals' colours,
   Deep in the woods
deer at times are seen;

The valley noon:
one can hear no bell,
   But wild bamboos
cut across bright clouds,
   Flying cascades
hang from jasper peaks;

No one here knows
which way you have gone:
   Two, now three pines
I have leant against!

'Visiting a Hermit and Not Finding Him' is a very common
theme in Chinese poetry. Critics regard this as one of the
earliest of Li Po's more famous poems, placing it variously
when he was seventeen or nineteen years old. Such a poem
is not just 'an excuse for a nature poem' but relates in its
thought to the 'spirit-journeys', of which Li Po himself was
particularly fond and which are to be found in early Chinese
poetry such as the *Ch'u Tz'u* (see Introduction, p. 60); even
though no fantasy is here expressed or implied. Making present
to the imagination the relationship of things in the landscape
itself is as much the spiritual meaning as any guess that the
reader may make regarding the hermit's whereabouts. Another

very simple poem on the same theme is one of the most famous in the language, by Chia Tao (777–841):

> Under a pine
> I asked his pupil
> Who said: 'Master's
> gone gathering balm
>
> Only somewhere
> about the mountain:
> The cloud's so thick
> that I don't know where.'

In such poems the wise hermit gives his 'teaching without words' (or, more correctly, 'teaching without telling') by letting the poet wait and not even meet him. His lesson may be compared with that of Ludwig Wittgenstein in *Philosophical Investigations*: 'Don't think: look!'.

ON HEARING A FLUTE
ON A SPRING NIGHT AT LOYANG

From whose house is it a clear flute
in the dark so flies its voice
it intermits Spring winds
filling Lo city?

For this evening among its airs
hearing 'Breaking the Withies',
who will not remember
long ago gardens?

Loyang (as in 'The Waters in the Rivers' in the Introduction, p. 65) was the eastern of the two great cities that served as capitals in the early Chinese dynasties, and second city of the Empire in T'ang times, when it had about 700,000 inhabitants.

'Breaking the Withies' is listed among twenty-four airs for the flute by the Han dynasty Academy of Music, the *Yüeh Fu* mentioned on p. 32. There was a custom then, and later, of breaking off withies, twisting them with difficulty from willows on the riverbank by a certain bridge outside the city of Ch'ang-an (the Early Han and the T'ang capital), as a symbol of reluctant parting. 'Long ago gardens' is a term for one's old home: 'Home, Sweet Home' may hardly be a respectable theme of contemporary European poetry, but it is one of the chief themes of all Chinese poetry.

静夜思

床前明月光　疑是地上霜

舉頭望明月　低頭思故鄉

QUIET NIGHT THOUGHTS

Before my bed
there is bright moonlight
So that it seems
like frost on the ground:

Lifting my head
I watch the bright moon,
Lowering my head
I dream that I'm home.

This must be the best known now of all Chinese poems, especially among Chinese overseas. (The reader will probably succeed in getting a friendly Chinese waiter to say it, in his own dialect.) The version here translates the one everybody knows, though the accepted version in Li Po's works differs slightly. I don't think the difference (if this is indeed not exactly how he wrote it) would worry him: 'time paints' perhaps also in poetry.

DRINKING WITH A GENTLEMAN OF
LEISURE IN THE MOUNTAINS

We both have drunk their birth,
    the mountain flowers,
A toast, a toast, a toast,
    again another:

I am drunk, long to sleep;
    Sir, go a little –
Bring your lute (if you like)
    early tomorrow!

The picture in this poem seems to me rather like a Nicholas Hilliard miniature. The lute, however, is a *ch'in*: a seven silk-stringed, half-tube zither; something like the modern Japanese *koto* which may be better known to readers. It is the most 'classical' of all Chinese stringed instruments, with a beautiful tone, and is mentioned as early as *Kuan Ch'ü* (p. 49 of the Introduction). It is also the symbolic 'lyre' of Chinese poetry (as in our word 'lyrical'); but with us the lyre has become only a symbol rather than an instrument to be played: these poets would have accompanied their recitals with a *ch'in*, and used it as an aid to composition. In indoor portraits of poets and scholars it is commonly part of the furniture; whilst in outdoor portraits it is often carried in a waterproof cover by a small boy behind the poet.

ABANDON

With wine I sit
absent to Night, till
(Fallen petals
in folds of my gown)

I stagger up
to stalk the brook's moon:
The birds are gone
and people are few!

This poem was referred to on p. 30 of the Introduction. It is
perhaps Li Po's most drunken poem and yet, in the original,
it is also a miraculous work of art. It seems to be a sort of reply
to a poem, famous for its spring freshness, by Meng Hao-jan;
though in no way a retort or a parody:

> In Spring one sleeps
> absent to morning
> Then everywhere
> hears the birds singing:
>
> After all night
> the voice of the storm
> And petals fell —
> who knows how many?

Meng Hao-jan, 689–740, was Li Po's chief hero among
poets of his own age.

On Marble Stairs
still grows the white dew
    That has all night
soaked her silk slippers,

But she lets down
her crystal blind now
    And sees through glaze
the moon of autumn.

This poem is translated in *Cathay* by Ezra Pound, with the title
'Jewelled Stairs Grievance'. (He makes it first person, but a
translator has complete choice in the matter since there are no
persons-of-the-verb in the original.)

The 'marble' of the Marble Stairs is 'jade' in the original but
has this meaning; and jade is also the epithet for a beautiful
woman's smooth skin. The 'white dew' thus suggests the
tears on her cheek, but White Dew is also the name of one of
the half-months (waxing and waning moons) in the Chinese
lunar calendar; being then the early part of September, and
giving a hint that the lady is no longer very young. The
'crystal blind' of course suggests the tears in her eyes, besides
being the name for a kind of roll-up bead curtain with rock-
crystals that she had in the Imperial Seraglio; to which
the Marble Stairs led.

She can therefore be recognized as an Imperial Concubine
who is losing the Emperor's attentions. Chinese Emperors
at the time had many concubines, the subject sometimes
of protest by the class of officials and poets who thought
the practice immoral; that is, against nature and so also
dangerous to the Tao of good government. The morality of
this was seen from the point of view of the girls; some of whom
would barely even meet the Emperor but still have to grow

old and lonely in his service. This was felt to be cruel and un-natural.

Li Po took the title of the poem and much of its imagery from a *chüeh-chü* by Hsieh T'iao, 464–99, whom he greatly admired, and of whom Shen Yüeh (Introduction, p. 89) had said 'We have not had poetry like this for 200 years!' The themes and, as it were, the furniture of Chinese poems are often repeated like this, in a way more familiar to us in painting (for instance almost all the furniture of 'On Hearing a Flute. . . at Loyang' on p. 107 is found also in a poem, but about autumn, by Tu Fu). This was not thought to subtract from the originality possible in a poem, any more than we should think a 'Still Life' or 'Portrait of a Lady' incapable of originality because these had been done before. The aim of such a poem was, like that of a painting, that it could be returned to often.

山中答俗人

問余何意棲碧山　笑而不答
心自閑　桃花流水杳然去別有
天地非人間

IN THE MOUNTAINS:
A REPLY TO THE VULGAR

They ask me where's the sense
　　on jasper mountains?
I laugh and don't reply,
　　in heart's own quiet:

Peach petals float their streams
　　away in secret
To other skies and earths
　　than those of mortals.

This is also called 'Question and Answer in the Mountains',
but the title given here seems to be the older. The visitor is
imagined as urging Li Po to forward his interests in the
intrigues at Court, in the capital. The 'peach petals' serve to
bring to mind the story of the Peach-blossom Cave, on p. 99,
and to make the poem one celebrating Imagination, not just
the landscape.

EARLY DEPARTURE FROM WHITE KING CITY

At dawn we leave White King,
    its clouds all coloured,
For passage to Kiang-ling
    in one sun's circuit:

While both banks' gibbons cry
    calls still unceasing,
Our light boat has gone by
    many fold mountains.

White King City, in the Yangtse Gorges, was a favourite resort in T'ang times. The distance to Kiang-ling, the burial place of the Kings of Ch'u in whose kingdom the *Ch'u Tz'u* (p. 60) were written, was well over 200 miles; but not impossible to cover, aided by the swift current, in twenty-four hours, of which there are true reports.

I think that, as with many Chinese river poems and river pictures, there is more than a suggestion in this of the journey of life ('its clouds all coloured' reminiscent of Wordsworth's 'trailing clouds of glory'); but it was not the custom of this age to make such things explicit or to point morals.

IN MEMORIAM:
GAFFER CHI, THE GOOD VINTNER
OF HSÜAN-CH'ENG

Vintner below by Fountains Yellow,
'Spring In Old Age', still do that vintage?
Without Li Po there on Night's Plateau,
Which people stop now at your wineshop?

'The Yellow Fountains' or 'Yellow Springs' (so called presumably because they are imagined as sulphurous and near a volcano leading to the underworld) is the Chinese name for Hades; for which the 'Terrace of Night' or 'Night's Plateau' is another. Wines in T'ang times often had the spring season in their names, and this sounds a typical name for a wine.

LETTER TO HIS TWO SMALL CHILDREN
STAYING IN EASTERN LU
AT WEN YANG VILLAGE UNDER
TURTLE MOUNTAIN

Here in Wu Land mulberry leaves are green,
Silkworms in Wu have now had three sleeps:

My family, left in Eastern Lu,
Oh, to sow now Turtle-shaded fields,
Do the Spring things I can never join,
Sailing Yangste always on my own –

Let the South Wind blow you back my heart,
Fly and land it in the Tavern court
Where, to the East, there are sprays and leaves
Of one peach-tree, sweeping the blue mist;

This is the tree I myself put in
When I left you, nearly three years past;
A peach-tree now, level with the eaves,
And I sailing cannot yet turn home!

Pretty daughter, P'ing-yang is your name,
Breaking blossom, there beside my tree,
Breaking blossom, you cannot see me
And your tears flow like the running stream;

And little son, Po-ch'in you are called,
Your big sister's shoulder you must reach
When you come there underneath my peach,
Oh, to pat and pet you too, my child!

I dreamt like this till my wits went wild,
By such yearning daily burned within;
So tore some silk, wrote this distant pang
From me to you living at Wen Yang . . .

Eastern Lu, where the children were at the home of their mother's family, is part of modern Shantung in North China; while Wu Land was the area round the mouth of the Yangtse, containing present-day Shanghai and Nanking and still in Li Po's day regarded as South China. Silkworms eat voraciously before spinning their cocoons, with three or in some breeds four rests, when the sericulturalist must be careful that they have absolute quiet. (Li Po might possibly be making some reference to his own creative activity.) 'Shaded' in 'Turtle-shaded' is the word Yin, of Yin and Yang; of which the turtle or tortoise is the symbolic beast, as the phoenix is for the Yang, There is here therefore an appropriate double meaning in mentioning the mountain. Li Po spent much of his time travelling, looking for patronage; which would usually mean travelling the great rivers as the main thoroughfares of the country. Where he was, the spring would of course be earlier than in the north.

The poem then enters into a 'spirit-journey' typical of many of his poems. The Tavern seems to be the name of part of the house, belonging to his wife's family, that he is said to have built on to, possibly not just for pleasure but as a business concern. There are various contemporary references to it, suggesting that it was thought remarkable, but none very informative. The 'one peach-tree' suggests his own imagination.

The writing of the poem on a piece of (raw) silk not only makes a connection with the silkworms of Wu, now spinning, at the beginning of the poem (where the introductory couplet before the quatrains is something quite commonly done) but has a punning origin, in that the word for 'silk' generally, even though not the one used here which means specifically 'raw silk', had the same sound as the word for 'thoughts'. ('Long silk' could mean something like 'longing thoughts'; which is perhaps the origin of the custom of surrounding peoples like the Tibetans, in giving silk scarves as symbolic presents.)

不向東山久薔薇幾度花
白雲還自散明月落誰家
我今攜謝妓長嘯絕人羣
欲報東山客開關掃白雲

1

Long since I turned
to my East Ranges:
How many times
have their roses bloomed?

Have their white clouds
risen and vanished
And their bright moon
set among strangers?

2

But I shall now
take Duke Hsieh's dancers:
With a sad song
we shall leave the crowds

And call on him
in the East Ranges,
Undo the gate,
sweep back the white clouds!

The East Ranges or East Mountain is in Chekiang province which at this date was called Yüeh; where the great Duke Hsieh An, A.D. 320–85, had lived in his youth and which he always loved. Hsieh An, with this love for his own countryside as well as for scholarship, but going to the aid of the nation in time of need, when he was responsible for a decisive victory over barbarian invaders, was the favourite Chinese type of hero. A story characteristic of him was that he was playing chess (*wei–ch'i*, usually known in the West by its Japanese name of *go*) when the news of the victory, won by his younger brother and a nephew commanding in the field under his directions, was brought to him; he glanced at the message, and went on with the game. Asked what it had contained, he said, 'Only that my boys have beaten the enemy'; but gave way to rejoicing when the game was over.

There is a legend, not apparently recorded until centuries after Li Po's own time, that this Duke recruited the beautiful dancing girls for his banquets from 'a rose grotto', as if they were really fairies, near his home in the East Ranges; but it seems at least possible that, rather than Li Po referring to this legend here, the legend might have arisen as an interpretation of this poem. 'Roses' are never mentioned in Chinese poetry of this date or earlier, so far as I can find, nor indeed much before recent Western influence; but this is one of four references to them in Li Po's poems: two of the others being to roses on a wall outside a window, and one to them growing on a rocky path; all of which seems strangely Western and un-Chinese, Chinese poetry having none of our symbolism of the rose in its tradition.

The origin of this symbolism, though very old in Greek poetry, seems to be Persian; the Greek name for the flower, from which our own comes through Latin, is certainly Persian in origin as well as other names in other languages. (The Chinese name looks as if it must be a loanword, too, but from what language is unknown to me.) It seems, therefore, that this poem of Li Po's, and his others mentioning roses, are among the rare instances where one can say there is something non-Chinese from the origins of his family, and his own birthplace, in the Far West.

The poem has been responsible for other problems in Li Po's works, such as a one-time belief that his own place of origin was the East Ranges (though he does not in fact say 'my' in the original, except by implication). The Duke Hsieh, too, most often mentioned in his works is not this one but his favourite poet, and one of the great pioneers of 'nature poetry' in Chinese – Duke Hsieh Ling-yün who lived in the fourth and fifth centuries and was a notable eccentric, also associated with Yüeh by Li Po; he will be met again in a later poem. Another Hsieh poet admired by Li Po, Hsieh T'iao, has already been encountered on p. 113. Problems concerning this little poem (a double *chüeh-chü*) therefore remain; but so also, unaffected, does the poem!

Three-sixty days with a muddled sot,
That is Mistress Li Po's lot:
In what way different from the life
Of the Grand Permanent's wife?

360 days is the length of the Chinese lunar year (periodically
brought in line with the solar year by the addition of a 'leap-
month'). It is nowadays called 'the farmer's year'.

The Grand Permanent was the short title for the high official
who during his term of office had responsibility for the ritual
purification of the Temple of the Imperial Ancestors, his own
life being expected to be one of monastic purity during his
term. One Grand Permanent, Chou Tse who was appointed
to the post in A.D. 67, became a byword for his excessive zeal.
When his wife, concerned to hear that he was unwell and
had taken to his bed, went to visit him he was so shocked at
this breaking of taboo that he had her imprisoned. The un-
fortunate man was then immortalized in a ditty that went the
rounds of the capital, to the effect that it could only be a bles-
sing for his wife not to see him on 359 days out of the 360;
to which someone added in rhyme that on the 360th it would
even be best for her to be 'muddled drunk'.

Li Po was four times married: two of his wives predeceased
him, from one there was divorce by mutual consent after a
very short marriage, and the fourth outlived him. A rhyme
like this, though, could be taken too seriously as evidence of
his marital life; as I fear it has been by some scholars. It could,
of course, have been addressed to the wife from whom there
was a divorce; but it may not have been, and may have been
the kind of spontaneous epigram in fun or apology that Li Po
would have been wiser not to let drop if he had known how
many centuries his fame would last.

THE BALLAD OF CH'ANG-KAN

(*The Sailor's Wife*)

I

I with my hair fringed on my forehead,
Breaking blossom, was romping outside:

And you rode up on your bamboo steed,
Round garden beds we juggled green plums;
Living alike in Ch'ang-kan village
We were both small, without doubts or guile ...

When at fourteen I became your bride
I was bashful and could only hide
My face and frown against a dark wall:
A thousand calls, not once did I turn;

I was fifteen before I could smile,
Long to be one, like dust with ashes:
You'd ever stand by pillar faithful,
I'd never climb the Watcher's Mountain!

I am sixteen but you went away
Through Ch'ü-t'ang Gorge, passing Yen-yü Rock
And when in June it should not be passed,
Where the gibbons cried high above you.

Here by the door our farewell footprints,
They one by one are growing green moss,
The moss so thick I cannot sweep it,
And fallen leaves: Autumn winds came soon!

September now: yellow butterflies
Flying in pairs in the west garden;
And what I feel hurts me in my heart,
Sadness to make a pretty face old ...

Late or early coming from San-pa,
Before you come, write me a letter:
To welcome you, don't talk of distance,
I'll go as far as the Long Wind Sands!

2

I remember, in my maiden days
I did not know the world and its ways;
Until I wed a man of Ch'ang-kan:
Now, on the sands, I wait for the winds . . .

And when in June the south winds are fair,
I think: Pa-ling, it's soon you'll be there;
September now, and west winds risen,
I wish you'll leave the Yangtse Haven;

But, go or come, it's ever sorrow
For when we meet, you part tomorrow:
You'll make Hsiang-tan in how many days?
I dreamt I crossed the winds and the waves

Only last night, when the wind went mad
And tore down trees on the waterside
And waters raced where the dark wind ran
(Oh, where was then my travelling man?)

That we both rode dappled cloudy steeds
Eastward to bliss in Isles of Orchids:
A drake and duck among the green reeds,
Just as you've seen on a painted screen . . .

Pity me now, when I was fifteen
My face was pink as a peach's skin:
Why did I wed a travelling man?
Waters my grief . . . my grief in the wind!

The second part of this ballad has long been rejected by many editors because of early traditions that it was not by Li Po but by one of several other poets of the eighth century. On the other hand, it was admitted by one critic, accepting these traditions because of their antiquity, that there was nothing in it that could not have been by Li Po and that was not also very good poetry. Modern critics are increasingly inclined to accept it as his work, and make of it (as it seems obviously to be even if it were not by his hand) a single two-part poem, together with the first part which all accept; intended to be, as they used to put on the silent screen, 'Later'. Perhaps this was such an original idea that it confused those not long after Li Po's time as to its authorship. Another cause of its rejection may have been a corrupt manuscript: the 1081 printed edition of his works gives it with considerable differences in places, which I think are inferior, but without listing variants as this edition usually does; presumably because they were unknown to the editors. Although various later collections of Li Po's poems excluded it, and many anthologies still do, there seems therefore no reason whatever to do so here. There is a famous translation of the first part of the ballad by Ezra Pound in *Cathay*, as 'The River Merchant's Wife: a Letter'.

The River Merchant or River Captain of the poem is, I think without a doubt, Li Po himself; so that the poem is a love-poem to his wife but written as if from her to him, which was a common Chinese practice at the time. Li Po, as has been remarked, spent much of his life travelling the Yangtse, and to say how much he missed her by saying how much she missed *him* would accord with convention.

In the first line, the meaning is '*first* fringed' on her forehead, making her about six. 'Round garden beds' in the fourth is literally 'round the bed' which was, besides meaning 'bed' itself, the term for the rail round the top of a well. The meaning is thus 'round the well', though I suspect that this was a colloquial term simply for 'in the garden', since every garden had a well in it. But the 'bed' obviously was also significant in the line, while 'green plums', the colour of youth and the earliest fruit, still today mean 'childhood love'. (The scene is, of course, imaginary, just as is Li Po's role as the river Captain.) Ch'ang-kan, probably already a good deal more than a 'village', was the port on the Yangtse of what is now Nanking.

There are two literary allusions in the fourth stanza: '*You'd* ever stand by pillar faithful' refers to a young man, Wei Sheng, of the sixth century B.C., who waited for his girl by agreement beside a pillar under a bridge; she never arrived, the river rose and he was drowned. '*I'd* never climb the Watcher's Mountain' refers to several stories and several mountains of this name, where ladies were supposed to have watched in vain for the return of their husbands. In the second line 'dust with ashes' implies 'impossible to separate'; no connection with our funeral service. (The young wife is sweeping in the next stanza but one. There is a 'broom' in the character for 'wife'.)

In the fifth stanza the Ch'ü-t'ang Gorge (near White King City, see p. 116) is one of the famous Yangtse Gorges, with the Yen-yü Rock like a Lorelei Rock in midstream and very dangerous to shipping especially in the monsoon. San-pa in the last verse is the three Pa districts also far away in Szechwan, while the Long Wind Sands is a Yangtse port itself a long way up-river from Ch'ang-kan.

In the second stanza of the second part, the Yangtse Haven was also some way up river from Ch'ang-kan, with the lowest bridging of the river and a port that gave its name to it (though in China it is more often called simply the Great River or the Long River). The Isles of Orchids in the fifth verse were fairy Islands of the Blest in the Pacific Ocean. The drake and the duck are mandarin ducks, symbols of conjugal fidelity; as now imagined by most Chinese in 'Kuan-kuan! Birds on river islands!' (Introduction, p. 49).

THE ROAD TO SHU IS STEEP

Heigh-ho! But it's hard!
And Hew! But it's high!

The Road to Shu is steep, steep as climbing to the Sky!

Ts'an Ts'ung and Yü Fu founded that nation
                Out of Disorder,
But when forty-eight thousand years later,
No hearth-smoke in sight back to their fastness
                From the Ch'in border,
West by Whitestar Fell (there were but bird-tracks)
Over Eyebrow Fell the Strong Men wandered,
                Earth they opened,
                Fells they sundered!

Then were sky-ladders fixed, bridges across chasms
That reach the mark where the Sun turns his Team of
  Dragons
And stretch far below to the swollen, swirling tor-
  rents:

            There, the yellow crane's flight
                cannot reach,
            Gibbons and monkeys moan
                as hands fail;

There, the Greenmire Way winding on and on
And taking nine turns every hundred steps,
I clutch for Orion, pass through the Pleiades,
                And gasp for breath;
    Then, beating my breast, I sigh,
                Sinking to Earth:

'Tell me, Sir, this Western Way, has it any end?
I fear its awful steepness, and can climb no more!'

I only see
Mournful birds,
Summoning mates
From ancient woods,
Cock follow hen
Into thicket,
And hear a cuckoo call
On moon to light
Sad, bare slopes . . .

The Road to Shu is steep, steep as climbing to the Sky!

It ashens those who only hear tell of it,
From its peaks to the sky can hardly be a foot:
The withered pines there have to lean over canyons
Filled with the contending dins of waterfalls,
Gullies thundering a thousand rolling stones!

Such perils, aye, as this,
Why, oh, why, Travellers from Afar, come ye to suffer
them?

Steep and stupendous
Pass of the Sabre
That one can defend
Against a thousand
And, be he No Friend,
Turn Wolf or Jackal:

'Ware tiger here!' from dawn,
From sunset, 'Serpent!
Teeth whetted to suck blood,
Kill like a sickle!'

Though told of Ch'eng-tu's charms,
Best homeward quickly . . .

The Road to Shu is steep, steep as climbing to the Sky!

I half turn, but gaze West; with a long, long sigh!

This is a *yüeh-fu* poem (Introduction, p. 31) with many changes of rhythm and with lines in the original varying in length from three to eleven syllables, some strongly rhythmic, others in themselves indistinguishable from prose, running and walking. In its own language it is in effect a musical composition, and it is still one of the most famous of all Li Po's poems despite the great changes in the sound of the language since his day.

As for its exact meaning in places, where there is some chaos in the syntax, and as a whole poem, it has always puzzled critics; some of whom have done their best to give it allegorical meanings, among them that it was a warning to the Glorious Monarch against his flight to Shu (modern Szechwan) in 756 during the An Lu-shan Rebellion – this despite the fact that the poem is already found in a T'ang anthology three years before that event!* It has always been difficult in the Chinese tradition to see any poem as other than occasional or in some way allegorical (which possibly this poem still is), but it may have been no more than the musical and visual composition that it remains, combining flights of supernatural imagination and mythology with natural description and unheroic down-to-earthness; its language ranging from rich archaisms to plain colloquialisms, all with complete originality. Perhaps no poem of the time shows better its boldness and energy, and 'Renaissance' spirit.

Ts'an Ts'ung and Yü Fu were mythical rulers of the Kingdom of Shu, gods of silkworm-breeding and of fishing. Ch'in is now the neighbouring province of Shensi, the king of which was in the third century B.C. to conquer all China and establish the first central government of the Chinese Empire (our name 'China' coming from Ch'in through Indian languages). 'Whitestar Fell' translates the name of T'ai-po Mountain on the borders of Ch'in and Shu; in which T'ai-po means 'very white' but is also the name of the planet Venus, and the T'ai-po of Li T'ai-po, Li Po's own style (second personal name

*A detail of a painting of this, probably contemporary but in an eleventh-century copy, is reproduced as the cover of this book.

bestowed on maturity). 'Eyebrow Fell' is the sacred O-mei mountain to the south in Shu. 'The Strong Men' were five heroes of Shu sent in legend to the King of Ch'in to bring back his five beautiful daughters for the harem of the King of Shu. On the way back, they saw the tail of a great serpent protruding from a cave and all seized it and pulled, until after a long struggle they at last dragged the creature out; whereupon the great mountain split open with terrible earthquakes, leaving the wild rugged country you will find there now. The Sun rides in a chariot drawn by a team of Six Dragons, and high in these western mountains is the signpost where he turns away on his journey at the end of the day.

The Sword or Dagger Pass, or 'Pass of the Sabre', is in the mountains between Ch'in and Shu, and 'No Friend' means both an outlaw and a supernatural fiend. Ch'eng-tu, or the Brocade City, is the capital of Szechwan (Shu) on the Brocade River; so called from a legend of a pious lady who washed in it the filthy robe of a Buddhist monk who had had the misfortune to fall into a dunghill. No sooner had she dipped the robe into the water than the river filled with bright flowers; which is said to be the origin of the industry of making lovely silk brocades, that continues in the district to this day.

The last line of the poem makes the gesture familiar in Chinese mime of a half-turn and a sigh. It is not made explicit whether the poet continues the journey or turns back.

THE BALLAD OF YÜ-CHANG

A Tartar wind blows on Tai horses
Thronging northward through the Lu-yang Gap:

Wu cavalry like snowflakes seaward
Riding westward know of no return,
Where as they ford the Shang-liao shallows
A yellow cloud stares faceless on them;

An old mother parting from her son
Calls on Heaven in the wild grasses,
The white horses round flags and banners,
Sadly she keens and clasps him to her:

' "Poor white poplar in the autumn moon,
Soon it was felled on the Yü-chang Hills" –
You were ever a peaceful scholar,
You were not trained to kill and capture!'

'How can you weep for death in battle,
To free our Prince from stubborn bandits?
Given pure will, stones swallow feathers,
How can you speak of fearing dangers?

'Our towered ships look like flying whales
Where the squalls race on Fallen Star Lake:
This song you sing – if you sing loudly,
Three armies' hair will streak, too, with grey!'

In the original 'Ballad of Yü-chang' of about the second or
third century, a white poplar is felled to become a pillar for
the Imperial Palace; where it sings a song of farewell to its
leaves and branches left on the hillside.*

*Arthur Waley, at the beginning of the Introduction to his transla-
tion of *The Book of Songs* (see Introduction to this book, p. 45), makes
the observation: 'Early Chinese songs do not as a rule introduce a

The Tai horses were a breed, largely of greys, from the Tartar borderlands of North China: there is an implication in 'blows' of blowing a trumpet, summoning them homeward. The action of the poem is in Wu, South China, by the great Poyang Lake in Kiangsi of which 'Fallen Star Lake' is part. The poem must have been written in 757, when the Glorious Monarch's sixteenth son, the Prince of Lin gathered a fleet in this neighbourhood, ostensibly to fight An Lu-shan's rebels but in fact also with personal ambitions to seize the throne himself. Li Po, unaware of this, joined him enthusiastically, suddenly convinced in his fifty-seventh year that military prowess had been his great hidden talent for serving the Empire all along. For this, when the Prince's treason was exposed and his feeble attempt at a *coup* crushed, the poet was later condemned to death; the sentence was commuted to banishment, on the way from which he died after a pardon.

Yü-chang was the home of his last, fourth, wife who is therefore given the role of the old woman singing the Yü-chang ballad as he goes off to war; but, by the usual convention, the poem is imagined as in the Han dynasty. 'Given pure will, stones swallow feathers' is an allusion to the great scourge of the Huns, Li Kuang (d. 125 B.C.), whom they called 'The Flying General' and whom Li Po claimed as an ancestor. This General, drunk one night, saw in the grass near his tent what he took to be a crouching tiger. He drew his bow with all his might and shot it. Next morning he found that it was only a white stone; but that his arrow had gone through it, feathers and all! He then tried, soberly and unsuccessfully, to repeat the feat.

---

comparison with "as if" or "like", but state it on the same footing as the facts they narrate'; and he quotes a Polish song which seems to have much in common with the old 'Ballad of Yü-chang' sung by the mother in Li Po's poem:

> They have cut the little oak, they have hewn it;
> It is no longer green.
> They have taken away my lover,
> Have taken him to the wars.

The old man's dream of military glory, assisted by the bottle, and his unwitting attachment to the forces of a thoroughly disreputable minor rebellion, were pathetic; but the poem that his imagination made, with its yellow and grey wintry scene, has a quite different kind of pathos: a poem against war, compassionate to all men and women.

HARD IS THE JOURNEY

Gold vessels of fine wines,
    thousands a gallon,
Jade dishes of rare meats,
    costing more thousands,

I lay my chopsticks down,
    no more can banquet,
And draw my sword and stare
    wildly about me:

Ice bars my way to cross
    the Yellow River,
Snows from dark skies to climb
    the T'ai-hang Mountains!

At peace I drop a hook
    into a brooklet,
At once I'm in a boat
    but sailing sunward . . .

(Hard is the Journey,
Hard is the Journey,
So many turnings,
And now where am I?)

So when a breeze breaks waves,
    bringing fair weather,
I set a cloud for sails,
    cross the blue oceans!

The Journey in the title and in the fourth verse is the Journey
of Life. The title, some of the detail and much of the spirit of
Li Po's poem (in three parts, of which this, though commonly
taken on its own, is the first) are all derived from ancient songs,

but especially from a later, long poem by Pao Chao (c. A.D 421–63). Pao Chao was one of Li Po's favourite poets, with whom Tu Fu compared him in a well-known poem; and was an important precursor of much in T'ang poetry, especially in his development of the seven-word metre as a form for serious composition. His poem is one of melancholy thoughts of happier days of the Empire, of his own disappointed ambition, and apparently of a broken marriage (though that, too, may be political symbolism), mingled with defiant gaiety. Li Po's in its entirety (some of it now very obscure) is somewhat similar; but his prologue is most remembered, as one of his clearest expressions of contempt for worldly ambitions (many see 'being drawn to the Court' as one of the meanings in 'sailing sunward') and of his doctrine of escape through the imagination. At the same time, the whole prologue seems to have something of the form of the Yellow River itself; the river, as so often, symbolizing the course of man's life.

沐浴子

沐芳莫彈冠浴蘭莫振衣
處世忌太潔至人貴藏暉
滄浪有釣叟吾與爾同歸

'Bathed in fragrance,
do not brush your hat;
Washed in perfume,
do not shake your coat:

'Knowing the world
fears what is too pure,
The wisest man
prizes and stores light!'

By Bluewater
an old angler sat:
You and I together,
let us go home.

'You and I' is addressed to the old angler who has spoken;
meaning that his advice is after Li Po's own heart. The story
is a very ancient one, referred to proverbially in the book of
Mencius who lived from *c.* 372 to 289 B.C.; though in his
version it is a young lad fishing who speaks. Although not
explicitly quoted here, in all versions the fisherman says: 'I
wash my feet in the muddy water, but I wash my hat-strings
in the clear water'; meaning that one must accept and cannot
escape from the 'muddy' world; yet can and must retain a
part of oneself unsullied by it – a saying not altogether remote
from 'Render unto Caesar the things that are Caesar's, and
unto God the things that are God's'. But Li Po is referring
particularly to a poem, probably of the third century B.C., in
the anthology the *Songs of Ch'u* (see Introduction, p. 60). In
this Ch'ü Yüan (343–290 B.C.), 'father of Chinese poetry'
by virtue of being the first named poet of importance and the
author of the great and exceptionally long poem 'Encountering
Sorrow', meets the old fisherman. Ch'ü Yüan is to the Chinese
the archetype of the incorruptible and faithful minister,

repeatedly wronged by his royal master; and his suicide at last by drowning in the Mi-lo River is still commemorated every year throughout China by the Dragon Boat Festival.

He is a Confucian hero, but the old fisherman's song that Li Po quotes is Taoist in spirit: Ch'ü Yüan is made to walk dejectedly along the riverbank, before drowning himself, lamenting his treatment and singing his own virtues and his aloofness from the corruption of the world; in a very smug way, that the Taoists make the Confucians adopt when they want to attack them. This the old fisherman does in his song (see David Hawkes, *Ch'u Tz'u, Songs of the South*, Oxford University Press, 1957, p. 90). It is Ch'ü Yüan, in the song, who says that after washing one's hair one *should* brush one's hat, and after bathing one *should* shake (out) one's coat; this Li Po makes the old fisherman contradict, though in the old song the latter only replies with the remark about clear and muddy waters, and then, in the Taoist manner, vanishes and says no more. (The Taoists always give themselves the last word, or the last silence, in this uncomfortable way for the Confucians.)

Without direct reference to it, or conscious thought of it, there is probably always some *latent* association with this story in the favourite Chinese image of the fisherman, whether in painting or poem, for example in 'River Snow' by Liu Tsung-yüan (A.D. 773–819):

> Among mountains
> where birds fly no more
> Nor have the paths
> any men's tracks now,
>
> There's orphaned boat
> and old straw-hat man
> Alone fishing
> the cold river snow.

The fisherman is the artist.

Did Chuang Chou dream
he was the butterfly,
   Or the butterfly
that it was Chuang Chou?

In one body's
metamorphoses,
   All is present,
infinite virtue!

You surely know
Fairyland's oceans
   Were made again
a limpid brooklet,

Down at Green Gate
the melon gardener
   Once used to be
Marquis of Tung-ling?

Wealth and honour
were always like this:
   You strive and strive,
but what do you seek?

This is one of a series of fifty-nine 'Old Poems' (more literally 'Ancient Winds' but with that meaning) which Li Po seems to have written at various times throughout his life, based on classical sayings and stories such as the one here of Chuang Chou (or Chuang Tzu) dreaming he was a butterfly (Introduction, p. 36). Fairyland's oceans being turned to a limpid brooklet refers to a fairy story; and the Marquis of Tung-ling was a high official who served under the Ch'in dynasty but retired to grow melons outside the Green Gate of Ch'ang-an, the capital, when Ch'in was overthrown by Han in the third century B.C. The statement, logically, is therefore quite true, even though it seems to apply to the melon gardener there now. This kind of paradox had great appeal to the Taoists.

A SONG OF ADIEU TO
THE QUEEN OF THE SKIES, AFTER A
DREAM VOYAGE TO HER

Seafarers tell of the Fairy Isles
Hid in sprays of great seas, not easily sought;
  Yüeh people say the Queen of the Skies
Can for moments be seen in a rainbow's light,
Risen high in the air beneath Heaven's Yoke,
Overawing Red Rampart, above the Five Peaks;
Where Heaven's Terrace, forty-eight thousand feet,
Faces, as if it would fall, towards the South-East:

  To dream my way to Wu and Yüeh
  I flew the other night over Mirror Lake;
  Mirror Lake's moon, chasing my shadow,
  Saw me as far as the Darting Brook;
And the Mansion still stood of the good Duke Hsieh,
Where his green waters rushed and his gibbons wailed;

There the Duke's climbing clogs I took for my feet
For I too would ascend his blue cloud ladder;
And I saw, from half-way, Sun spring from the sea,
Heard Heaven's Cock himself crow down from
    Heaven!
But in a thousand crags my way was unclear
Till, lost in wild flowers in those scars and ghylls,
I reclined on a rock: suddenly dark fell
And bears growled, dragons howled, waterfalls
    thundered,

      Affrighting the forests,
          aye,
      And the piled-up peaks!

The clouds were black, black,
　　　　aye,
And the rain would come!

The waters still, still,
　　　　aye,
And making mists!

Then lightning flashed,
　　Thunder rolled,
　　　And peaks collapsed!
And, guarding Heaven's Grotto,
　　The rock split in two
On a great blue cavern: I could see no ground
Sun *and* Moon on the roofs of silver and gold!

Rainbows their raiment,
　　　　aye,
The winds for their steeds!

Her Cloud Princesses,
　　　　aye,
Came riding in train!

Her Lutenists tigresses,
　　　　aye,
Phoenix drawing her Car!

And all her Fairy Folk,
　　　　aye,
Were like fields of flax!

*

My spirit was startled,
　　my senses were stirred,
With such awe upon me
　　that I sighed aloud;

Then woke to find nothing
　　but pillow and quilt,
And lost was that Vision
　　of Vapour and Cloud
(And so Joys go for ever, where here below
The waters in the rivers all Eastward flow!)

　　　　　*

O Queen, I must leave you,
　　　　aye,
But when to return?

Upon this green hillside
　　I'll keep a white deer
To ride, when the time comes,
　　to your Glorious Peaks!

For how can I drop my glance, bow my waist to the
　　　　Great,
Who will never let me show my true heart or true face?

This is a *yüeh-fu* poem in varied rhythms, and otherwise in
many ways similar in style to 'The Road to Shu' on p. 129.
In parts it closely imitates the *Ch'u Tz'u* (Introduction, p.
60), including phrases divided by the 'sigh', which I have
translated as 'aye'; but also in places it is quite close to modern
colloquial.

'The Queen of the Skies', T'ien-mu, more literally 'Heav-
en's Matron', is the name of a mountain in Chekiang (Yüeh
in these poems) but in the third line, of course, means the Fairy
Queen herself. 'The Fairy Isles' in the first line are the same as
'the Isles of Orchids' in the Ballad of Ch'ang-kan and 'Fairy-
land' in the Old Poem (pp. 125 and 141). 'Heaven's Yoke' is the
constellation Auriga, the Waggoner. 'Red Rampart' is the
name of a famous mountain; the Five Peaks are the five sacred

mountains of China; and 'Heaven's Terrace' is another mountain range; all of these far from one another geographically.

In the second stanza, Duke Hsieh is the fourth–fifth century poet Hsieh Ling-yün mentioned in the note on p. 122. He was a keen mountaineer and invented a detachable and reversible sole with studs or cleats to put on his boots: the short studs in front and the long ones behind for going uphill, the other way round for coming down. (There is some gain in grandeur but loss in adventure, when one reads in the history that he was accompanied in his mountain-climbing by 700 retainers!) As has been said, he was one of the first of Chinese 'nature poets' and a favourite of Li Po's, and also was a notable eccentric. One endearing story is of his liking for wearing the clothes of bygone centuries, and having his servants wear the same; in which on one occasion he made a magisterial progress to one of the towns in his district, causing the inhabitants to bar their doors and windows in the belief that it was the Devil himself who was approaching with his retinue. But he was always happy, and known as 'Happy Hsieh'.

The Sun springs up out of the Pacific Ocean before dawn, its rays first lighting the top of the Heavenly Tree; whereon sits Heaven's Cock who gives the signal to the cocks on earth, which is still in darkness, to crow.

The 'great blue cavern: I could see no ground' must inevitably remind the reader of another 'spirit-journey', Coleridge's *Kubla Khan*; of which in other ways this poem is reminiscent, not least in its literary allusions (which are more numerous than suitable to detail in these notes). 'My spirit' and 'my senses' translate respectively two different words for 'soul': exclusively human and shared with the animals. The quotation from 'The Waters in the Rivers' (see Introduction, p. 65) is not exact in the original, but the same proverb in different words. The 'white deer' is a Taoist symbol often seen in paintings: the animal ridden by the Immortals.

The end of the poem seems also to have an affinity with the end of *Kubla Khan*, even though quite differently expressed,

in giving the romantic poet's notion of Society's view of
himself:

> And all should cry, Beware! Beware!
> His flashing eyes, his floating hair!
> Weave a circle round him thrice,
> And close your eyes with holy dread,
> For he on honey-dew hath fed,
> And drunk the milk of Paradise.

To me at least, this seems to match Li Po's own thought so
well, and to be such a perfect ending to Coleridge's famous
poem, that I now find it difficult to believe in the interruption
by the 'person on business from Porlock'.

日色欲盡花含烟月明如素

愁不眠趙瑟初停鳳凰柱蜀

琴欲奏鴛鴦絃此曲有意無

人傳願隨春風寄燕然憶君

迢迢隔青天昔時橫波目今作

流淚泉不信妾斷腸歸來看取

明鏡前

LONGING

Sunlight begins to fade,
    mist fills the flowers,
The moon as white as silk
    weeps and cannot sleep,

Chao zither's Phoenix frets
    no more shall I touch,
Shu lute's Mandarin Duck strings
    I'll sound instead:

This song has a meaning
    that no one can tell,
It follows the Spring wind
    as far as Yen-jan

To you far, far away
    beyond the blue sky –

Whom once I gave
A sideways glance
With eyes that now
Are wells of tears –

If you do not believe
    that my heart breaks,
Come back and look with me
    into this glass!

The title of this poem (which Li Po also uses for another, quite
unconnected poem) is literally something like 'long' or 'far-
away thoughts of one another', and is the phrase that made
the pun with 'a long piece of silk' (see p. 119). A man, as has
been said, commonly wrote a love-poem as from the woman;
here a professional courtesan and musician.

'Chao zither's Phoenix frets' and 'Shu lute's Mandarin Duck strings' are taken in many commentaries to refer to decoration on the instruments (both of which are in fact kinds of zither in the original); but doubting this interpretation I enquired of Dr Picken, who provided the music for the songs in the Introduction and who remarked in his reply: 'I do not believe the remarks about decoration; I think *Feng-huang* (Male and Female Phoenix) and *Yüan-yang* (Mandarin Drake and Duck) are balanced pairs of harmonising entities.'

COMING DOWN FROM
CHUNG-NAN MOUNTAIN
BY HU-SZU'S HERMITAGE,
HE GAVE ME REST FOR THE NIGHT
AND SET OUT THE WINE

At dusk I came down from the mountain,
The mountain moon as my companion,
And looked behind at tracks I'd taken
That were blue, blue below the skyline:
You took my arm, led me to your hut
Where small children drew hawthorn curtains
To green bamboos and a hidden path
With vines to brush the travellers' clothes;
And I rejoiced at a place to rest
And good wine, too, to pour out with you:
Ballads we sang, the wind in the pines,
Till, our songs done, Milky Way had paled;
And I was drunk and you were merry,
We had gaily forgotten the world!

This is typical of Li Po's occasional poems, a 'bread-and-butter
letter' to a friend who had entertained him. The 'hermitage'
is not to be taken too seriously, and need mean no more than
a country cottage. In a world of intriguing courtiers, everyone
was pleased to be called a retired hermit; though the word used
for 'hermit' here is in fact also a high Taoist Degree of Initia-
tion. ('The world' at the end of the poem, though a fair trans-
lation of the word used, translates something that can itself
mean 'intrigue'.)

Last year we made war for the Mulberry Brook's
   springs,
This year we make war for the Garlic Stream's bed,
We have washed our swords in Antioch's waves,
We have grazed our mounts on the Pamirs' snows,

For thousands of miles our expeditions go
Till the Three Armies' men are worn and old,
But the Huns look on killing like tilling their fields,
White bones all they grow on their yellow sands!

House of Ch'in built the Wall to keep them apart,
House of Han has to keep the beacons alight,
Beacons alight and they never go out
For these expeditions have never an end:

In the line, hand to hand, they'll die the same,
The horses will fall, call to Heaven their pain,
The crows and the kites pick their riders' guts
And fly to dead trees with the bits in their beaks ...

Where Captains and Men paint the grasses red
Our General's without a plan in his head:
You surely know war's an ill-omened tool
That never was used except by a fool?

'We fought (for the) South of the Walls, we died (for the)
North of the (Earth) Works' is the beginning of a Han dynasty
ballad translated by Arthur Waley, 'Fighting South of the
Ramparts', in his *Chinese Poems* (1946). Many other poems
were called after it in later ages. The tune, probably lost even
by Li Po's time, was one of 'Eighteen Airs for Songs to Pan-
pipes and Cymbals' listed by the original Han Academy of
Music (see note on p. 32); and the opening lines quoted are

typical of dance-songs the world over in having no more precise meaning than, say, Tennyson's 'Cannon to right of them . . .' The line was so famous, however, that an ancient scholastic work gave it a mystical meaning: the Imperial *City* (the same word as for *wall*) was at the exact median point between Heaven, symbolized by the South towards which the throne faced, and Earth, symbolized by the North; the Emperor having the divine mandate to mediate between the two!

'Brook' and 'stream' in the first two lines are rather free (the Mulberry River is in the far North-west and the Garlic River is the Pamir River), but Li Po seems to mean the names to sound trivial and absurd. 'Antioch's waves' meant, at least in Han times when the poem is by convention set, the Mediterranean itself. To Li Po, however, it may have suggested both somewhere very remote, like 'Timbuctoo', and the name of another place similarly transcribed into Chinese, in the Far West of his own birth. The Pamirs in the translation stand inaccurately for the T'ien Shan, Celestial Mountains, which now divide Chinese from Soviet Turkestan.

The Huns, in Chinese Hsiung-nu which may be cognate with our name, were a warlike, nomadic people of Central Asia, similar in way of life though probably not exactly the same as the Hunnish tribes who invaded Europe in the fifth century. The Wall is, of course, the Great Wall, about 1,500 miles long (or twice that, with all its twists and branches) and mostly first built in the Ch'in dynasty, third century B.C., by forced labour including political prisoners. The beacons were a sign of a state of war: their failure to light at ordained times indicated that a post had fallen to the enemy.

The crying horse and the carrion crows are details of the old ballad, but Li Po gives them a Goya-like horror even greater in his own visual and compact language.

The reader may find it interesting to compare this anti-war poem with Tu Fu's on p. 167, as well as with another of Li Po's own on p. 133. Effective as both of Li Po's poems are in making vivid the cruelty of war, neither can really be described as a 'political poem' as neither suggests any positive policy. This one may vaguely advocate a 'Maginot Line' policy; but for all its strength of language it is politically rather incoherent, compared with Tu Fu's anti-war poems which pointed to particular scandals or errors in policy about which something could and should be done. One clear point of policy, however, the two poets certainly had in common: disapproval of the expansionist policies that the dynasty was beginning to pursue and which led, in 751, to a disastrous defeat of Chinese armies by the Persians and Arabs; and indirectly to the weakening of the central, civil power.

'The Three Armies', in this poem and in that on p. 133, is an ancient expression for massive forces: it has been used currently in a poem by Mao Tse-tung. The last couplet is from the Book of Lao Tzu, or Tao Te Ching, the oldest and greatest of the Taoist Classics (translated by D. C. Lau, Penguin Books, 1963).

ON SEEING CUCKOO FLOWERS AT
HSÜAN-CH'ENG

In Shu Land I have heard what the cuckoo calls,
At Hsüan-ch'eng I have seen the cuckoo flowers
  once more:
Let him call once, but once, at once my heart will break,
For the Spring thrice, Moon thrice, and thrice for
  San-pa!

The Chinese cuckoo is particularly associated with Szechwan
(Shu Land), an exiled Prince of which was in legend turned
into one so that he might return each year (like Proserpine).
Its call is heard by the Chinese as '(it's best to) go home!' –
'(pu ju) kuei ch'ü', in which the 'kuei ch'ü' in Li Po's day
would have sounded 'kui k'ü' in tones that matched well the
cuckoo's notes. (Readers may have observed that these notes
also give an extraordinarily good 'homing': one can turn at
once to the point they come from.) The cuckoo to the Chinese
is therefore the bird of homesickness.

The cuckoo flowers are a kind of spotted azaleas, also
associated with Szechwan; the home of rhododendrons and
azaleas whence they came originally to the West. Hsüan-
ch'eng, where Li Po was, is in Anhwei province, far from
Szechwan; so that the sight of azaleas there moved him to
write this little song, which is like a cuckoo's call itself: many
of his poems are as natural in the original as birdsong.

'Moon thrice', besides being like 'three cheers for the
Moon' (and Spring and San-pa in Szechwan), means the third
month, that is, April in the Chinese calendar; the cuckoo's
month. Chinese poets, as we have seen, are very fond of
making expressions mean two or more things at once: a
quality of all poetry, to which their language is well suited.

三五七言

秋風清　秋月明　落葉聚還散
寒鴉棲復驚　相思相見知何日
此時此夜難為情

THREE, FIVE, SEVEN WORDS

The autumn wind is light,
The autumn moon is bright;
Fallen leaves gather but then disperse,
A cold crow roosts but again he stirs;
I think of you, and wonder when I'll see you again?
At such an hour, on such a night, cruel is love's pain!

The poem is called 'Three, Five, Seven Words' because that is
the metrical pattern in the original (a word being a syllable).
These lengths of line are all ones appropriate to the classical
poetry (*shih*) of the time; as which the poem is therefore
regarded, rather than as one of the new, syllabically irregular
song-lyrics to contemporary music (*tz'u*: see Introduction,
p. 34). Apart from its metrical originality it is also close to the
developing *tz'u*, of which Li Po is credited with writing a few
examples, in its particular lyrical spirit as a love-song.

THE WATERFALL ON LU MOUNTAIN

When, west, I climbed Incense Brazier Peak,
I southward saw curtained cataracts
Suspend their stream some three thousand feet
Then roar through dales several miles away;
Sudden as if flying lightning came
But mystic, too, as white rainbows rose:
At first I feared Milky Way had dropped
And sprinkled stars, falling through the clouds!

As I looked up they increased in force,
So mighty was the Creator's work:
An ocean wind blew there without cease,
The river moon gave skies back their light,
The skies in which random torrents rushed;
To left and right the green walls were washed
By flying pearls scattering light mist
And streaming foam boiling round great rocks!

Let me travel to those Glorious Peaks
Where I may feel peace grow in my heart:
I'll have no need more for magic draughts
For I may there wash dust from my face
And enjoy there lodging that I love,
Ever parted from the world of men!

The Lu Mountain, about 5,000 feet high, is in Kiangsi province
about six miles south of Kiukiang, and an especially sacred
place to the Taoists. Those who have visited it say that,
though now covered with villas and teahouses, and very

'touristy', it is one of those places which still retain a deeply spiritual quality.

The 'white rainbows' in the first stanza mean the effect of light shining through the curtains of water. In the second stanza in particular, I think one can see something of the 'scientific' quality of Li Po's mind; and I suspect that the expressions he uses in this and other of his 'nature' poems have a good deal more meaning of this kind than is now generally understood or than can be brought out in translation. (The 'ocean wind', for example, is the perpetual 'cosmic wind' going round the world; and 'random torrents', as I have translated it, probably has more meaning than just a figure of speech.) 'The Creator' in this and other Chinese contexts does not mean our God; but the Master Craftsman who made the Universe in harmony with the Tao, which came before him and which is nearer to our God.

This poem (Li Po also compressed the imagery of the first verse into a *chüeh-chü* with the same title) is, to this day, the subject of many landscape paintings, with the tiny figure of the poet on a rock under the waterfall; but besides such direct references to it, it seems to contain the whole spirit of later Chinese landscape painting, which in turn influenced Chinese gardens, and they in their turn our own English gardens and new attitude to nature from the end of the seventeenth century; the English watercolour school of the eighteenth century and the romantic movement itself in Europe.

Needless to say, it is not suggested that all this came from this poem, or from Li Po (Wang Wei, himself a painter – see p. 94 – was probably a much greater influence in China and ultimately abroad); but it is interesting at least that 'sprinkled' and 'falling', *sa* and *lo*, in the eighth line make up the first two syllables of what has been suggested was the original of the strange 'Chinese' term *sharawadgy* used by Sir William Temple in his *Gardens of Epicurus* (1683) for a quality of naturalness – this book had a profound influence on the new English gardening, derived from China, coming through the Netherlands, where Sir William was Ambassador, and falling on the fertile ground of Classical notions of Arcadia. The notion in this *sa-lo* was that of Heraclitus, of the ever-changing yet never-changing waterfall as the symbol of nature; a reason for the special importance of waterfalls in Chinese paintings. Another reason, I think, is that they help one to *hear* the paintings.

TU FU

AT AN EVENING PICNIC,
WITH YOUNG BUCKS AND BEAUTIES ON
CHANG-PA CANAL, IT RAINED!

1

Sunset's the time to take the boat out
When a light breeze raises slow ripples,
Bamboo hidden is the picnic place
And lotus fresh in the evening cool;

But while the bucks are mixing iced drinks
And beauties snow a lotus salad,
A slip of cloud comes black overhead:
Before it rains my sonnet must end!

2

It *has* rained too, soaked those on the seats
As a squall rose to beat the boatside,
The girls of Yüeh wear wet scarlet skirts
And those from Yen weep tears of eyeblack:

The painter peels its bough on the bank,
The curtains curl and flowers strew the foam;
All the way home there's a howling storm
And on the shore is Autumn-in-June!

A pair of lighthearted *sonnets* (see Introduction, p. 93), not precisely datable but believed by critics to be from the 740s. These and the next, serious poem are the only ones in the present selection from before the An Lu-shan Rebellion, described in a note to come. The young bucks were sons of prominent people in the capital; the beauties professional, like *geisha*. The Chang-pa Canal was opened only in 741, so perhaps was still something of a toy for gilded youth. There are several light touches of the mock-heroic here, as in the storm; and in the 'wet scarlet skirts', the point of which is rather lost if it is not recognized as a parody of typical poetic hyperbole (to which Tu Fu himself was very partial) for heroines soaking their dresses with tears.

The ice for the drinks would have been dug out of mounds, where it was buried in winter; but 'snowing' a lotus salad, which was shredded lotus root, may mean no more than rinsing it. There would have been an awning on the boat, much as in Impressionist paintings of pleasure-boats on the Seine, so that it took the squall to give the girls their worst wetting: Yüeh, modern Chekiang south of the mouth of the Yangtse, is still famous for its pretty girls; as also is Yen, the region round modern Peking. In old poetic tradition the two were extremes of south and north.

Summer poems are comparatively uncommon in Chinese, for reasons evident in this one: because of the monsoon the season is very hot and wet, and so not much liked.

It is a strange thing about Tu Fu that even such a youthful and summery poem as this seems in retrospect to take on something of the prophetic concerning his own times and his own life. It is known that he kept all his poems carefully in the order of their composition from his early childhood; and he may quite consciously therefore have seen them in continuity rather like the long scroll-paintings of rivers, which divide into separate landscapes and which were an invention of his own epoch.

originally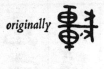

later 車

ch'e
chariot, cart,
waggon

originally 馬

later 馬

ma
horse

[see overleaf]

車轔轔馬蕭蕭行人弓箭各
在腰耶孃妻子走相送塵埃不
見咸陽橋牽衣頓足闌道哭
哭聲直上干雲霄道傍過者
問行人行人但云點行頻或從
十五北防河便至四十西營田

THE BALLAD OF THE ARMY WAGGONS

The din of waggons! Whinnying horses!
Each marcher at his waist has bow and quiver;
Old people, children, wives, running alongside,
Who cannot see, for dust, bridge over river:

They clutch clothes, stamp their feet, bar the way
    weeping,
Weeping their voices rise to darkening Heaven;
And when the passers-by question the marchers,
The marchers but reply, 'Levies come often:

'They take us at fifteen for up the river,
To garrison the West, they'll take at forty,
Your Headman has at first to tie your turban,
Grey-headed you come home, then back to duty –

'The blood that's flowed out there would make a sea,
    Sir!
Our Lord, his lust for land knows no degree, Sir!
        But have you not heard
Of House of Han, its East two hundred regions
Where villages and farms are growing brambles?

'That though a sturdy wife may take the plough, Sir,
You can't see where the fields begin and end, Sir?
That Highlanders fare worst, they're hardy fighters
And so they're driven first, like dogs and chickens?

  'Although you, Sir, ask such kind questions,
  Dare the conscripts tell their wretchedness?
  How, for instance, only last winter
  The Highland troops were still in the line
  When their Prefect sent urgent demands,
  Demands for tax, I ask you, from where?

So now we know, no good having sons,
 Always better to have a daughter:
For daughters will be wed to our good neighbours
When sons are lying dead on Steppes unburied!

    'But have you not seen
      On the Black Lake's shore
The white bones there of old no one has gathered,
Where new ghosts cry aloud, old ghosts are bitter,
Rain drenching from dark clouds their ghostly chatter?'

Though sometimes translated as 'The Ballad of the Army *Chariots*', this would be an anachronism by about 1,100 years: cavalry was introduced, replacing chariots in war, about 350 B.C.; and this poem is dated towards the end of the year A.D. 750. It is one of several famous poems, and is probably the most famous, written by Tu Fu about this time against war and particularly against the scandals of press-ganging methods of recruitment; some of which were illegal, like making men do more than one period of national service such as is implied in this poem. Tu Fu, when he later became a local Commissioner of Education (a job he found most frustrating, and hated), had to set examination questions to test local candidates for higher education and then higher civil service posts; and among the questions he set was one about recruitment for national defence, and how the candidate would take account of the needs of agriculture. The concern felt by Tu Fu, in contrast with Li Po, for such practical matters has already been men-·tioned in the note on p. 154 to the latter's famous 'We Fought South of the Walls'.

Like Li Po, Tu Fu has followed the convention of setting his poem in the Han dynasty ('Our Lord, his lust for land' refers to the great conquering Emperor, Han Wu-ti, who reigned from 140 to 87 B.C.). He has also written it in the tonally 'free' metres of the old ballads, with their kind of language and such devices as concatenation; as in '. . . bar the way weeping,/Weeping their voices rise . . .'. But, unlike Li Po, Tu Fu had no ancient model, and both title and poem are entirely of his own creation.

Tu Fu starts his poem with a six-syllable line, a practice common in ballads with an effect like a fanfare, before breaking into the seven-syllable metre; the syntax of which, more than anything else, gives the original a marching rhythm. This, which could easily become merely monotonous, is interrupted by insertion of formulaic phrases, in the old ballad style, like 'But have you not heard . . .?' Such phrases point up as well as break the main rhythm, rather like the exclamations in 'hot-gospelling' services; as also does the passage of *recitative*, out of the main metre, from 'Although you, Sir' to 'Always better to have a daughter', before the marching rhythm is returned to. These lines have the effect of being urgent and confidential, not to be overheard; and the resumed marching then seems fatalistic.

'Highland' translates the high plateau of Ch'in (see note on p. 131), the modern province of Shensi, Tu Fu's own province and the area round the then capital, Ch'ang-an which is now Sian-fu. It is typical of Tu Fu to be concerned about the way the families of these soldiers, traditionally the best in the Empire, were being dunned for tax while their men were away at the front. He may also have been worried, as there was good cause to be later, about the depletion of the defences around the capital.

The Black (or Dark Blue) Lake is Kokonor, the great salt lake more than 10,000 feet above sea-level in Northern Tibet. There were campaigns here as well as 'up the river' (the Yellow River) in 750.* But, as with Li Po, the mention of such distant places also implied militaristic policies of a dangerous kind; which indeed they proved to be, most of all through the power they allowed the generals to acquire within the nation.

*Kokonor and the upper reaches of the Yellow River are mentioned in many poems of the time, as scenes of incessant fighting; rather like the North-west Frontier of India in our Imperial days.

Tu Fu may have thought of the old ghosts, at the end of the poem, as those of the Han dynasty in which it is fictionally set; but the new ghosts as those of yesterday and today: with a hint of the ultimate fate of the Han dynasty, when it gave way to warlordism which was followed by nearly four centuries of short-lived dynasties, some of them foreign, ruling the different parts of a divided empire.

His chilling, atmospheric ending is characteristic.

In the present century Mr Shui's father, a mining engineer working in this area, used wherever he could to pay to have the white bones still to be found there properly buried by the locals; who regarded him as rather eccentric for doing so, claiming that some at least were only those of yaks and camels.

LOOKING AT THE SPRINGTIME

In fallen States
hills and streams are found,
Cities have Spring,
grass and leaves abound;

Though at such times
flowers might drop tears,
Parting from mates,
birds have hidden fears:

The beacon fires
have now linked three moons,
Making home news
worth ten thousand coins;

An old grey head
scratched at each mishap
Has dwindling hair,
does not fit its cap!

This is a sonnet, in the same syllabic metre as the pair of sonnets on p. 163, though rhymed in the translation and also differently written out. It was composed by Tu Fu in the enemy-occupied capital, Ch'ang-an, during the spring of 757, when the city was filled with the Tartar troops of the rebel Central Asian general An Lu-shan. (Lu-shan, his personal name, in modern Cantonese Lok-san, is related to that of Alexander the Great's wife Roxana, who was a Bactrian.)

The reign of the Glorious Monarch, Ming Huang or Hsüan Tsung (born 685, reigned 713–56, died 762), had begun with his seeming a model of Confucian puritanism and rectitude. Administration, communications and education were all improved beyond any precedent; the arts and sciences were encouraged and seemed to burst with an entirely new life (even now, as of fifteenth-century Florence, it seems incredible that so many great men were alive at the same time); and there were justice, peace and prosperity everywhere as never before, for about a quarter of a century. This has ever since been looked on by the Chinese as a golden age, indeed above all others of their history; and has meant no less to other beneficiaries of their civilization, such as Korea, Japan and Vietnam. Without a realization of all this, an understanding of the disaster that was to follow, and of much in Tu Fu's poems, is impossible. The story must therefore be briefly told.

The decay seems to have started in the 730s, when, after the death of his favourite concubine, the middle-aged Emperor was at first inconsolable, increasing the austerity which he had already introduced to court life. But he was then induced to expropriate the young wife of one of his sons, the Lady Yang Yü-huan, who is known to history and literature under her later imperial title as Favourite Concubine, Yang Kuei-fei. Apart from her beauty, which was well-rounded in the robust taste of the T'ang arts, she was, like the Emperor himself, an accomplished musican; and for the rest of his life, even after her death, his love for her seems to have obsessed him utterly and to the point of madness.

Yang Kuei-fei may have had thoughts of the throne one day for herself, with the precedent of the great Empress Wu in the previous century. Her own relatives and others she favoured grew constantly in power, and the once puritanical and peaceful Emperor became increasingly extravagant and politically interested only in military glory for his armies.

In the 740s he was persuaded more or less to retire; as if his life's work were now done and he could give himself to pleasure, in the confidence that all was well in the hands of those he had so wisely chosen. The cost of the military adventures and of the new splendour of his court led to increased taxation and discontent among his people; while officials who had served him (and them) faithfully were ousted, and the new class of official took self-enrichment for granted. Junior officers, without what they considered adequate opportunities for this, saw no hope of promotion except through 'influence': if not in the present Emperor's court, then in some rebel's that might replace it.

Among the court favourites at the time was General An Lu-shan, who had achieved some military successes. He was short, exceedingly fat, and jolly, and soon became a sort of court jester, delighting the Emperor. His mother had been a Turkish sorceress and he may well have been valued also for his know-ledge of the occult, in which the Emperor was more and more immersed.* Yang Kuei-fei, with the Emperor's permission, adopted him as her 'son'; and gifts were lavished on him, including military governorships and the choice of many of the Imperial Stables' best horses: all providing him with re-sources for his rebellion in December 755. In a couple of months he had taken Loyang, the Eastern Capital, and there proclaimed himself Emperor of a new dynasty; but he then suffered a number of reverses, culminating in a major defeat on 1 July, which seemed as if it might herald an end to the rebellion.

By 9 July, however, palace interference had succeeded in reversing the situation again: Yang Kuo-chung, Prime Minister and cousin of Yang Kuei-fei, had cast doubt in the Emperor's mind about the resourcefulness and even loyalty of the able general who had successfully been defending the pass to the Western Capital, Ch'ang-an; the seat of the Emperor himself and of his government. Eunuchs were despatched to command this general to break out of his sound defensive position in the pass and, against his military judgement, to attack the supposedly weak rebel force facing him. As a result, his army entered an enemy trap of which he had long been aware. Of 200,000 loyal troops (Tu Fu exaggeratedly calls it 'a million' in a poem to follow), mainly Highlanders of Ch'in,

*There is something in common, in character and historic role, between An Lu-shan and Rasputin; a resemblance strengthened by the fact that the murderers of both found them uncannily difficult to despatch.

only 8,000 ever returned; the pass was open to An Lu-shan's forces, and Ch'ang-an beyond it.

At dawn on 14 July 756, the Emperor secretly fled from the capital with Yang Kuei-fei, her cousin the Prime Minister and her ennobled sisters, a few other princes and princesses, advisers, eunuchs, and a party of soldiers. On the discovery of their departure, panic and looting broke out in the great city (it had at that time about a million inhabitants), and the Prefect sent his respects to An Lu-shan in Loyang, as Emperor; delivering the city up to him, and so trying in vain to prevent the fearful massacre which followed the arrival of the Tartar troops.

Although An Lu-shan himself was killed in the following year by a number of his courtiers, including an ambitious son, and the main rebellion and its side rebellions were eventually all defeated so that the T'ang dynasty was to last in name for another 150 years, there was never again the good government, peace and prosperity there had been in the first twenty-five years of the Glorious Monarch's reign. The powers that had been granted the military, in the form of military governor-generalships of provinces in order to put down the rebellion, were never given back; and some parts of the Empire were ever after virtually the independent kingdoms of local war-lords.

The Emperor's fleeing party, meanwhile, stopped on the morning of 15 July to change horses at a post-station beside the River Wei (pronounced Way), about forty miles west of Ch'ang-an. There some of the soldiers crowded round the Prime Minister, Yang Kuo-chung, to demand more food. Others, at a distance, saw the scene, concluded he was plotting with them, drew their bows and shot him dead. The Emperor's advisers then realized that the loyal officers and men involved, on whom his life and theirs depended, would never feel safe so long as the Prime Minister's patron and cousin, Yang Kuei-fei, lived. The Emperor was told, and pleaded; but at last a eunuch led her out of the station building to a pear-tree by a Buddhist oratory, and there strangled her. Her body was shown to the troops, who cried 'Long live the Emperor!';

and the arduous journey westward to Szechwan was continued, after the brief enactment of a scene that was to become the centre of countless Chinese (and Japanese and other) stories, poems and plays.

Tu Fu, a middle-aged minor civil servant, was absent from Ch'ang-an at the time of its fall; but by the autumn was in the enemy-occupied capital. How he came to be there is not known; the events, whatever they were, for once not being recorded in his poems. It is generally supposed that he must have been captured by a party of rebels and taken by them, perhaps as a porter, to the capital. He was not of sufficient importance to be otherwise of interest to them; or, fortunately, even worth killing. It would be in character for him to feel no desire to make a poem about such a pitiful and only personal matter.

In this poem, instead, he says something universal about the situation in which he found himself, and about all sorrow: both objectively and subjectively observing the unreasonable-seeming unconcern of Nature at such times. The second verse is difficult to translate because of what seems 'double-grammar': a feature in Chinese poetry that contributes to its quality of 'faceted jewels', as it is put by the great French sinologue, Paul Demiéville (see Introduction, p. 84); who says he often had occasion to sing this poem to himself during the enemy occupation of his country during the Second World War.

This verse can be construed both as if it meant 'the flowers only cause my tears to drop; parted from my family and friends, the sight of the birds only increased my anguish'; and as translated here, I think. If I am right (the phenomenon is not uncommon in this language and is rather like 'There's anguish in the birds' might be in an English poem), the two interpretations would be simultaneous rather than separable; while each would develop the thought in the first verse and at the same time perfectly observe 'verbal parallelism' in this one, in accordance with the requirements of the form. (It will be noticed that in this sonnet there is verbal parallelism also in the first verse, which begins in the original 'states fall . . .' followed by 'cities spring', as a verb meaning 'have spring': here the parallelism is voluntary.)

As David Hawkes says in his *Little Primer of Tu Fu*: 'It is amazing that Tu Fu is able to use so immensely stylized a form in so natural a manner. The tremendous spring-like compression which is achieved by using very simple language with very complicated forms manipulated in so skilful a manner that they don't show is characteristic of Regulated Verse at its best.' ('Regulated verse' is the usual English name for what this book, and Hawkes elsewhere, calls the Chinese 'sonnet'.)

In the third verse, which of course also has the same prescribed verbal parallelism, 'beacon fires' indicates a state of war; rather like searchlights on the horizon nowadays, and as already encountered in Li Po's poem on p. 152. 'Three moons' means three months of *this* year; placing the poem in the third Chinese month, that is to say April. The 'three moons' make a verbal and visual parallel with the 'ten thousand [gold] coins'.

The last verse is not literally translated: this is not in order to achieve the rhyme, which could be as easily done in a literal translation, but because of what seems too great an oddity to have the kind of impact on modern Western readers that it would have had on Tu Fu's. It is not in fact a 'cap' that Tu Fu's wrily mocking self-portrait refers to, but a 'hatpin' that would not now secure his official bonnet. At the time he would probably be wearing a simple 'coolie-hat' or headcloth, but a gentleman and official (the two were, theoretically at least, synonymous) of his day would wear his long hair in a topknot, through which a pin could secure the bonnet. (Pigtails, hated by the Chinese, were forced on them by the Manchus in the seventeenth century.)

In the Introduction to his *Anthologie de la poésie chinoise classique* (Éditions Gallimard, 1962), Paul Demiéville gives a transcription of this poem as it would have been pronounced in Tu Fu's day; this is copied below with slight changes in the spelling to suit the English reader, and written out in the same way as the translation. The mark — over a vowel means that the syllable is in what this book calls a 'tense' tone; and the mark ᴗ that it is in a 'slack' tone. These also indicate the dominant vowel in a diphthong or triphthong. The bracketed syllables are in positions where there is licence to have the 'wrong' tone; otherwise the reversals of tone will be seen to make a perfect pattern:

> Kuĕk p'uă,
> shān hā dz'ăi;
> Zhiēng ch'ūen,
> ts'ăo mŭk shēm;
>
> (Kăm) zhī,
> huā tsiĕn luĭ;
> Hĕn b'iĕt
> tieŭ kiāng siēm:
>
> (P'uōng) huă,
> liēn sām nguăt;
> Kā shō,
> tiĕi muăn kiēm:
>
> (B'ăk) d'eū,
> sāo kăng tuăn;
> Hŭen iuŏk,
> pŭet shēng chēm.

The old man from Shao-ling,
　weeping inwardly,
Slips out by stealth in Spring
　and walks by Serpentine,

And on its riverside
　sees the locked Palaces,
Young willows and new reeds
　all green for nobody;

Where Rainbow Banners once
　went through South Gardens,
Gardens and all therein
　with merry faces:

First Lady of the Land,
　Chao-yang's chatelaine,
Sits always by her Lord
　at board or carriage,

Carriage before which Maids
　with bows and arrows
Are mounted on white steeds
　with golden bridles;

They look up in the air
　and loose together,
What laughter when a pair
　of wings drop downward,

What bright eyes and white teeth,
　but now where is she?
The ghosts of those by blood
　defiled are homeless!

Where limpid River Wei's
    waters flow Eastward,
One goes, the other stays
    and has no tidings:

Though Pity, all our hours,
    weeping remembers,
These waters and these flowers
    remain as ever;

But now brown dusk and horse-
    men fill the City,
To gain the City's South
    I shall turn Northward!

This poem was composed about the same time as the last, also
in the enemy-occupied capital. (More will be said about its
date and possible circumstances below.) It is in the style of an
old ballad, like Coleridge's *Ancient Mariner* to which its sixth
and seventh verses seem to come rather close in poetic imagery.
At the same time, it develops the theme in the last poem, of
Nature's indifference to human sorrow; and makes existence
amongst nothing but this indifference the terrible fate of the
'homeless ghost'. Then, typically of Tu Fu, in the last verse it
changes course back into the world of the living.

    Ballad features include, in the original, a deliberately
archaic-sounding series of imperfect rhymes; as well as the
favourite concatenations and the device, found in ballads the
world over, of the 'flashback'. (An old man in Iceland once
said to the author: 'When I was young, the ballads were our
cinema!') The reader will notice the way in which Tu Fu brings
this 'flashback' forward again, identifying the 'limpid River
Wei' with where he is by the Serpentine.

    This (David Hawkes's translation of the name gratefully
borrowed) was an artificial lake resembling a winding river and
much like the Serpentine in London. As it had been made for

the Emperor Wu-ti of Han in the first century B.C., the style of the poem is suited to it. The Rainbow Banners were imperial standards, and the South Gardens were hibiscus gardens in the south of the park containing the lake. (All that remains now of all this is a marshy depression.)

Chao-yang was the name of an imperial palace in Han times, and its chatelaine indicates the beautiful Lady Fei Yen (Flying Swallow), consort of the Emperor Ch'eng-ti who reigned from 32 to 5 B.C.; standing, of course, for Yang Kuei-fei. The Maids of Honour, leading the way for the imperial carriage and carelessly shooting from their white steeds, are undoubtedly Yang Kuei-fei's sisters; for whom, unlike Yang Kuei-fei herself, nobody ever had a good word to say.

There is an old saying: 'A brace of birds' (expressed as 'a pair of wings') 'with one arrow'; which Tu Fu has varied by the use of a character rather similar to 'arrow' but meaning 'laugh'. The two characters both have 'bamboo' in them: 'laugh', it is said, because a man laughing shakes like the leaves of bamboo.

The bird or birds brought down so gaily may be said to symbolise the worthy ministers of the Emperor, who were banished or executed as a result of the sisters' intrigues; but the image is not effective merely as clever allegory or for its moral which could, like Coleridge's, be opposition to blood sports: its meaning, like his, is in the language of poetry.

The last verse of the ballad returns to earth. It has occasioned many difficulties for commentators, unhelped by attempts at emendation; and can only be understood now by reference to a map of eighth-century Ch'ang-an. reconstructed from excavations. The great walled city covered 30 square miles,* its walls running due north and south, and east and west. The park with the Serpentine was in the south-east corner; but *protruded* out of the near-perfect square of the city, *southward* for more than half a mile. In the South Gardens of it, therefore, Tu Fu in order 'to gain the City's South' would indeed have

* Rome in A.D. 300 covered just over 5¼ square miles. Ch'ang-an is said to have been the biggest walled city ever built by man.

to 'turn Northward'; but he would not have ended his ballad with so trivial a remark and no other meaning to it.

On part of this meaning most commentators agree: that he was somehow looking to 'the Emperor in the North', Su-tsung, who had succeeded his father, the Glorious Monarch, on the latter's abdication after the events by the River Wei; and who had been in the 'North', about 400 miles north-west of Ch'ang-an at the time, although he was by now 100 miles west of Ch'ang-an at Feng-hsiang, which is the place Tu Fu eventually escaped to. He would still, however, have been called 'the Emperor in the North', thus distinguished from 'the Emperor in the West', the retired Glorious Monarch in Szechwan; and the (usurping) 'Emperor in the East', the son of An Lu-shan who himself had by now been murdered. Reference to the geography shows that Tu Fu could be expressing by an apparently harmless remark his intention to escape and return to Ch'ang-an with the eventually victorious Emperor Su-tsung.

But the question remains: was it harmless to be where he was at all, to which he had 'slipped out by stealth'? And where he 'walked secretly', by a closer translation? The possibility therefore remains that he means that he was already on his way. He is known to have escaped by some time before the end of May, and although that would be summer by Chinese reckoning, his reference to 'spring' need hardly have an exact temporal meaning, any more than in Mao Tse-tung's poem on p. 97.* The first part of this final verse, more exactly translated, means that he had seen the yellow or brown dusk over the city, and 'the dust of the Tartar horsemen' filling it; who had probably come to supervise the curfew: possibly a good moment to escape out of the city and one would think a very bad one to creep back into it. (Where he was, he was already outside the city wall.)

*There is not intended to be an implication in any of this reasoning that Tu Fu must have composed the poem then and there. Neither, of course, need this verse be taken as a wholly circumstantial, rather than imaginative, account of his escape.

This is, of course, mere conjecture; but it would not be un-characteristic of Tu Fu to express his adventure so laconically; just as he seems not to have told of his other adventure, his original capture, at all. The autobiographical nature of Tu Fu's poems tends to disguise the fact that they were all first and foremost poems. His view of poetry, in the Confucian tradi-tion, was wider than 'art for art's sake'; but, within his wider concept, it was still poetry for poetry's sake.

From THE JOURNEY NORTH:
THE HOMECOMING

Slowly, slowly we tramped country tracks,
With cottage smoke rarely on their winds:
Of those we met, many suffered wounds
Still oozing blood, and they moaned aloud!

I turned my head back to Feng-hsiang's camp,
Flags still flying in the fading light;
Climbing onward in the cold hills' folds,
Found here and there where cavalry once drank;

Till, far below, plains of Pin-chou sank,
Ching's swift torrent tearing them in two;
And 'Before us the wild tigers stood',
Had rent these rocks every time they roared:

Autumn daisies had begun to nod
Among crushed stones waggons once had passed;
To the great sky then my spirit soared,
That secret things still could give me joy!

Mountain berries, tiny, trifling gems
Growing tangled among scattered nuts,
Were some scarlet, sands of cinnabar,
And others black, as if lacquer-splashed:

By rain and dew all of them were washed
And, sweet or sour, equally were fruits;
They brought to mind Peach-tree River's springs,
And more I sighed for a life misspent!

Then I, downhill, spied Fu-chou far off
And rifts and rocks quickly disappeared
As I ran down to a river's edge,
My poor servant coming far behind;

There we heard owls hoot from mulberry leaves,
Saw fieldmice sit upright by their holes;
At deep of night crossed a battlefield,
The chill moonlight shining on white bones:

Guarding the Pass once a million *men*,
But how many ever left this Pass?
True to orders half the men in Ch'in
Here had perished and were alien ghosts!

I had fallen, too, in Tartar dust
But can return with my hair like flour,
A year but past, to my simple home
And my own wife, in a hundred rags;

Who sees me, cries like the wind through trees,
Weeps like the well sobbing underground;
And then my son, pride of all my days,
With his face, too, whiter than the snows,

Sees his father, turns his back to weep –
His sooty feet without socks or shoes;
Next by my couch two small daughters stand
In patched dresses scarcely to their knees

And the seawaves do not even meet
Where old bits of broidery are sewn;
Whilst the Serpent and the Purple Bird
On the short skirts both are upside-down!

'Though your father is not yet himself,
Suffers sickness and must rest some days,
How could his scrip not contain some stuffs
To give you all, keep you from the cold?

'You'll find there, too, powder, eyebrow black
Wrapped in the quilts, rather neatly packed.'
My wife's thin face once again is fair,
Then the mad girls try to dress their hair:

Aping mother in her every act,
Morning make-up quickly smears their hands
Till in no time they have spread the rouge,
Fiercely painted great, enormous brows!

I am alive, with my children, home!
Seem to forget all that hunger, thirst:
These quick questions, as they tug my beard,
Who'd have the heart now to stop and scold?

Turning my mind to the Rebel Camp,
It's sweet to have all this nonsense, noise . . .

This is an extract, exactly half the length of the whole 'Journey North', written about October 757; which, with 140 lines, is a very long poem by Chinese standards, and one of the longest of Tu Fu's. These are lines 21–90: the first twenty lines being an apology for leaving the service of the new Emperor at the temporary capital, Feng-hsiang, in order to visit his family whom he had not seen since he was captured a year before; and the last fifty lines being a review of the future problems for the final restoration of the dynasty to its former, and an even greater, glory. This account of the journey itself and of his arrival home to his family is one of the best-loved passages in all his works. The poem is written in five-syllable 'old style' verse (that is to say, tonally free), which is the most favoured form for long poems and, in effect, the Chinese epic metre.

Tu Fu had for a few months at Feng-hsiang held the only appointment close to the throne he was to have in his life, and it had not been altogether successful. He had been, at a junior

level, one of those whose duty it was to write minutes 'remind-
ing' the Emperor of things he was going, in his infinite wisdom
to do; which was, of course, a euphemistic way of describing
the task of advising and even admonishing a sacred being. Tu
Fu, with Confucian notions of the Ideal Monarch, or rather
of the ideal civil servant, and with great moral courage, took
his duties seriously; on one occasion he went so boldly to the
defence of a colleague whom the Emperor disliked that he
made the Emperor lose his temper and came near to losing
his own head. (Tu Fu's apology, on escaping with his life,
still pleaded for the man.) At the same time, being no prig, he
wrote poems observing and laughing at his zeal. The Emperor,
however, was probably very glad to have him go on leave;
and it seems to have been clearly understood that he would not
be returning.

Tu Fu's art of narration is shown at its best in this poem.
While room is allowed for leisurely observation and an
impression is given of distance covered, the journey itself is
greatly foreshortened (from Feng-hsiang in the second stanza
to Pin-chou, already 'far below' in the third, for instance
would have been about seventy-five miles of travel on foot
through still dangerous country); and the device of the
soliloquy about the disastrous Battle of the Pass (itself a long
way off his route, in fact) is used to bring the journey,
while still far from home, to a timely end for the sake of the
poem.*

In the third stanza, 'Before us the wild tigers stood' is not a
true literary allusion, but borrowed diction from two or three
sources. It indicates wild country. 'The Peach-tree River's
springs' refers to the famous story told by T'ao Yüan-ming
(see Li Po's poem and the note on p. 99). The fieldmice by
their holes sat with folded arms out in front of them (at least
in Tu Fu's imagination), thus in the posture of the temple

*Tu Fu's introduction of the Battle of the Pass into this poem, as
if he were at the site of it, may be sufficient hint, truthful as he was by
nature, not to take all his statements as circumstantial truth, including
his account of his escape in the last poem.

guardians seen in sculpture. The little creatures were there-
fore guarding their holes, just as the men of Ch'in in the next
stanza had guarded the Pass, but foolhardily against the owls
– birds of ill omen to the Chinese.

Tu Fu's family at the time consisted of his wife, his son
whom he called by the pet name of 'Pony', two small daugh-
ters, and a baby boy about a year old, whom he called by the
pet name of 'Bear' and who had been born during his
captivity, so that Tu Fu had not yet seen him. The seawaves
on the little girls' skirts will be familiar to anyone who has
seen a 'mandarin coat'; while the Serpent only freely translates
the name of the official in the heavenly bureaucracy, with a
tiger's body, nine human faces, eight feet and eight or ten
tails, who was responsible for the waters; and who is also
identified with the Spirit of the Valley in Taoism. The Purple
Bird is the Phoenix. A typical touch is the delay implied by
'next by my couch' while the little girls ran to dress up before
seeing their father. Probably all possessions that were acceptable
to the pawnbroker had disappeared from the house.

The red eyebrows that the little girls gave themselves with
their mother's make-up would seem to the Chinese to make
them like demons.

FOR WEI PA, IN RETIREMENT

Our livelong days we never meeting
Move as do stars in other clusters,
Yet this evening ('And what an evening!')
We're sharing this lamp and candlelight;
But youth and strength, how briefly it lasts
For both our heads have become grizzled
And half of those we ask about, ghosts,
Till cries of shock pierce our very breasts:
How could we know twenty years would pass
Before I came again to your house?
Though in those days you were unmarried
Suddenly sons and daughters troop in,
'Greet merrily Papa's Companion',
Ask from what parts it is that I come?
But such exchange remains unfinished:
You chase them off to get out the wine
'And in night rain pull up spring onions'
To be steamed fresh with yellow millet . . .
Now (with your 'Come, we can meet seldom')
You've charged my glass ten times in sequence:
Ten times and still I'm not quite tipsy
But filled with sense of old acquaintance;
For tomorrow the hills divide us,
Both out of sight in the world's affairs!

A large proportion of the work of all Chinese poets, great as
well as minor, consists of 'occasional' poems: 'bread-and-
butter letters' – poems such as this, which is one of the most
famous of its genre. (It may be compared with another, no less
famous, by Li Po on p. 151.) It was written in the spring of
759, when Tu Fu, who had not been brought back on to the

Imperial Staff, had the job of a local Commissioner of Education; but he appears at the time to have been sent by the Prefect of the District to Loyang, the Eastern Capital, now in Imperial hands again. (The main and original rebellion had by now been defeated, but serious side-rebellions and unrest were to continue for some years and, as already said, never entirely depart from the weakened dynasty's history.) It must have been on this trip that he took the occasion to visit his old friend in the poem, who is unidentified. ('Pa', meaning 'eight' and suggesting that he was an eighth child, would have been this friend's name within his own family and among intimates, not his official personal name.) 'In Retirement' means that he was a member of the official classes, but not at present in employment: such people, though they might be surrounded by family, servants and farmworkers on their estates, were conventionally referred to as 'living in hermitage'.

The poem is written in the same 'old style', tonally free metre as the last; though the 'tune' is not quite the same, particularly in not having the quatrain structure. The opening phrase, translated as 'Our livelong days', is a familiar 'formulaic phrase' in the old ballads, with the sound of folk music in it; so it at once sets the nostalgic mood of the poem, which is assisted by appropriate literary allusions. The 'stars in other clusters' are in fact two stars in constellations that would never be up at the same time, and so are often proverbially referred to as a symbol for two people being parted. 'And what an evening!' is from the refrain of a wedding song in the Book of Odes (see Introduction, p. 45). 'Greet merrily Papa's Companion' is from an ancient book of etiquette, which goes on to say that thereafter the children should be 'seen and not heard': something that, with Tu Fu's evident approval, these cheerful children did not observe.

'And in night rain pull up spring onions' is a literary allusion, or Chinese family saying. Like many such sayings in one's own family, it derives from a very simple story, so simple that one would hardly tell it to strangers: Kuo T'ai, A.D. 127–69, a famous scholar, teacher and 'character', on one particular occasion went out into his garden, although it was raining hard, to get some leeks, shallots or spring onions to make soup for a guest; that is all.

The drinking would then, in the custom of T'ang times, have taken place after the meal; so that the last lines of the poem portray the rest of the evening, and Tu Fu's thoughts on going a little unsteadily to bed.

There are, or should be, no rules about *how* a poem achieves its effect: in their originals, this poem and the one by Li Po just referred to are equal in their naturalness, and would equally have delighted their recipients. But it may be noticed that, whereas Li Po's poem is a flow of images with no particular form, Tu Fu's is, underneath and unobtrusively, constructed like a piece of architecture. It starts and ends with the two friends parted; the climax in the middle being the entry of the merry children. Each of its twenty-four lines, and for that matter forty-eight half-lines, is a unit of sense in this sym-metrical structure; and so, it almost seems, is every possible numerical factor: each couplet, each triolet, each quatrain and so on, looked at with its mirror reflection in the other half of the poem. Of course, one should not expect this to be exact, nor think of Tu Fu as a geometrician instead of a poet; but the reader may see for himself the truth of it, even in the translation where it cannot be quite as firm as in the original. Yet the original loses nothing in naturalness by its construction; and only prejudice, in those who believe that everything in art must be done as if by magic to its doer, could suppose that it did.

Tu Fu, by the way he speaks of him, very probably thought of Li Po as a magician, and himself as not; but he knew his own genius.

originally

later 春
水

ch'un shui
Spring (time)
waters

[see overleaf]

客至

舍南舍北皆春水　但見羣鷗日〻来
花徑不曽緣客掃　蓬門今始為君開
盤飱市遠無兼味　樽酒家貧只舊醅
肯與鄰翁相對飲　隔籬呼取盡餘杯

THE VISITOR

North and South of our hut
  spread the Spring waters,
And only flocks of gulls
  daily visit us;

For guests our path is yet
  unswept of petals,
To you our wattle gate
  the first time opens:

Dishes so far from town
  lack subtle flavours,
And wine is but the rough
  a poor home offers;

If you agree, I'll call
  my ancient neighbour
Across the fence, to come
  help us finish it!

This is another sonnet, in the seven-syllable metre in the
original. According to William Hung it was written in the
spring of 761.

    Later in the year 759, after the last poem was written, Tu
Fu had given up his post as a local Commissioner of Education
(which, as already remarked, he had much disliked) and moved
with his family to Ch'eng-tu (see note on p. 132), where he
lived by doing odd literary jobs and helped by donations
from patrons: as Li Po lived for most of his life. With money
gained and given he was able to build himself a cottage, also
one of those little riverside belvederes one sees so often in
Chinese paintings, on the Brocade River. Although he was
already in ill-health and probably consumptive (reasons,
among others, for his not at the time trying to get another

civil service job), this was one of the brightest and most peaceful stretches of his life's own river: as reflected in this sonnet and the nine short songs that follow. Tu Fu had immense capacity for happiness, and for what cannot be called by any more appropriate name than 'fun'; and clearly preferred this (in which not all poets are like him) to sorrow. It is this that makes his many sad poems so infinitely sadder than they might otherwise be; but at the same time makes his categorization as 'a sad poet' so wrong.

Tu Fu has a note on this sonnet, saying that the visitor welcomed in it was a 'Prefect Ts'ui'. This had been his mother's name, so his grand visitor may have been his uncle or some other relative on her side. She was a great grand-daughter of Li Shih-min, who had become the Emperor T'ai-tsung and who, though he had first put his father on the throne, was the real founder of the T'ang dynasty and one of the greatest men in the history of China. (Tu Fu's blood was, as it happens, extraordinarily 'blue': he was related to almost all the grand families in the Empire; but it does not seem to have done him any good in his career. Great people, Emperors especially, had very many children; and cadet branches of grand families rapidly became uninfluential and poor.)

The 'rough wine' in the poem is literally 'old wine'; but as a term in rice oinology, this means unclarified rice wine in the old-fashioned style before the method of clarification was invented.* This was the cheaper but also the stronger sort; and Tu Fu, though here he politely apologizes for it, preferred it. Though not a notorious drinker, like Li Po, Tu Fu was always a deep drinker and even speaks of this as something of an affliction from his early youth. By now, it is evident from his poems, his doctors were trying to get him to give up alcohol

*Grape wine was also drunk, and is mentioned in a famous poem by Li Po. It had been imported first in the Han dynasty from the West; and seems at that time to have been reserved by sumptuary laws for imperial use. But it seems that the rice wine could also be excellent; Marco Polo, from Italy, was to consider it 'better worth drinking than any wine of the grape'.

altogether for the sake of his health – which may have made him welcome the excuse for a party all the more.

As for the 'poor home', whilst Tu Fu was indeed poor (though not as poor as he had been or was to be again) he would have said it however rich he had been: it is again simply Chinese manners not to praise one's own; dignified and in no way self-pitying or begging. And there was no shame in poverty in Tu Fu's class.

NINE SHORT SONGS:
WANDERING BREEZES: 1

The withies near my door
    are slender, supple
And like the waists of maids
    of fifteen summers:

Who said, when morning came,
    'Nothing to mention'?
A mad wind has been here
    and broke the longest!

These nine short songs (*chüeh-chü*, see Introduction, p. 83) were written like the last poem in the spring of 761. 'Wandering Breezes' is a very free translation of the title; which could as well be 'haphazard or random inspirations, joys, felicities' or the like, but is really untranslatable. In most editions the song above is placed last; but one early edition places it as here, first, which surely must be right.

Tu Fu's short poems of this kind are much less well known than those of Li Po, with their special magic; but they should be judged in themselves and not by the kind of comparison that only reduces the enjoyment of both poets.

NINE SHORT SONGS:
WANDERING BREEZES: 2

You see your guest sit sad,
    sit sadly dozing,
Yet, shameless Spring, invade
    his river look-out:

Why fly these petals in
    in such profusion?
And need those orioles' songs
    be so insistent?

Both the petals and the orioles are symbols associated with pretty girls and love.

Peach and plum I put in
  were not ownerless:
The old boy's wall, though low,
  does mark a garden:

So like the winds of Spring
  by stealth to rob them,
At night to come and blow
  and break some blossom!

NINE SHORT SONGS:
WANDERING BREEZES: 4

Aware my working room
    is thatched and humble,
The river swallows come
    and go regardless:

Mud from their beaks on books,
    on lute their droppings,
Intent on midge pursuit
    they almost brush me!

As well as the books, the lute (in fact a *ch'in*, see note on p.
110) would be as much a part of a T'ang poet's equipment for
his work as a piano for a modern composer.

Broken the moon of March,
  April approaches:
Henceforth how many Springs
  am I to welcome?

No good thinking of things
  I've no account of:
Before life's dregs are drained,
  there's still some glasses!

NINE SHORT SONGS:
WANDERING BREEZES: 6

It tears my heart to see
River Spring ending,
Leaning on staff before
a fragrant island:

Willow catkins are mad
to follow those breezes,
Silly the peach's blooms
to sail such waters!

The word for 'breezes' here also means 'fashions', so Tu Fu
reproves the catkins and wild-peach petals in the role of an
old gentleman shocked by the 'young generation'.

NINE SHORT SONGS:
WANDERING BREEZES: 7

I'm lazy, have no job,
    won't leave the village,
Call my sons in the day:
    'Please shut the lattice!'

On blue moss, with rough wine,
    woods will be peaceful
(Spring winds on jasper brooks)
    outdoors this evening.

originally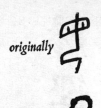

later

mu
mother

[see overleaf]

糝徑楊花鋪白氈點溪荷葉疊青錢筍根稚子無人見沙上鳧鶵傍母眠

NINE SHORT SONGS:
WANDERING BREEZES: 8

The catkins line the lanes,
   making white carpets,
And leaves on lotus streams
   spread like green money:

Pheasants root bamboo shoots,
   nobody looking,
While ducklings on the sands
   sleep by their mothers.

This seems to be what is going on outside, while Tu Fu is
having his siesta in the last song. These are willow catkins
again, which, though not in themselves white, would make
white carpets in the strong sunlight suggested.

On the west wall of my hut,
   leaves of mulberry;
In river fields, young wheat
   standing elegant:

Shall I see many more
   Springs turn to Summer?
But now I'll not forgo
   wine sweet as honey!

FOR YOUNG
GENERAL HUA CHING-TING
(A Song of Music in Brocade City)

The Brocade strings and reeds
  weave daily music,
Half of it with the clouds,
  half river breezes:

For music such as this
  was meant for Heaven,
How many times is Man
  allowed to hear it?

This poem, written in the autumn of 761 and similar in form to the 'Wandering Breezes', has in fact an underlying political and satirical content. The Brocade City was, of course, Ch'eng-tu. The story is that Tu Fu composed the song for a singing girl to sing at a banquet to the young General Hua Ching-ting, who is said also to have 'got the point'.

The young general had been achieving outstanding success (under the higher command of the same Prefect who had surrendered Ch'ang-an in 756 but had later escaped and greatly distinguished himself in the loyal cause) and had succeeded in recovering still rebel-held territory, at the head of an army of irregular troops which he had himself gathered together. This success was showing signs of going to the young general's head; so that there was a danger that he too, as so often happened, might become a rebel and have aspirations to the Celestial Throne ('Heaven'). What Tu Fu cannot have known at the time was that the young general had achieved his success by allowing his irregulars to loot freely and commit appalling atrocities. His commanding officer, the former Prefect, did not at the time know, either; but was to die of a broken heart when he learned the truth.

'Weave' in the translation is for a reduplicated adverb really of the opposite sense: *fen-fen*, which means 'unravelled', hence 'broadcast (into)'. That, since radio, could hardly be used, however; and there is also in the Chinese term a suggestion of *thread*.

ON SEEING A PAINTING OF HORSES
BY GENERAL TS'AO PA AT
SECRETARY WEI FENG'S HOUSE

Since our T'ang times began, in painting horses
We counted but one Prince inspired divinely,
Till this General won fame the past three decades
By presenting to Man a true Godly Creature:

He did His Late Majesty's 'White-at-Night' charger
And for days Dragon Pool lightened and thundered!
Court Ladies brought Command to Maids of Honour
That they fetch from deep vaults an agate trencher
To give to the General, who danced obeisance;
And there flew to his brush satins and damasks
From Kinsmen and Courtiers, to get its traces
So their screens might receive similar radiance!

From the past of T'ai-tsung a 'Curly Piebald'
And now the House of Kuo's own 'Dappled Lion'
Are in this new painting, and both such horses
As to set connoisseurs sighing with envy
(Or together in war, proof against thousands)
On a plain silk background, making a sandstorm;
While seven horses more, no less excellent,
Are done distant and cold, like snow at sunset:
Stamping their frosty hooves where tall catalpas
And grooms and stable boys make little forests!

All nine, marvellous beasts of Spirituality
And regard pure and proud, profound, courageous;
And who has loved such beasts more devotedly
Than Wei Feng recently or Chih Tun formerly?

They bring to mind a march East to the Palace
When there swept in those skies Kingfisher Banners
And there leapt, pranced and thronged three thousand
      horses
Like this painting, each one, in bone and sinew!

But since Tribute was paid to Father River
We shoot dragons no more from river waters:
                  Or have you not seen
At Golden Granary, in pine and cypress,
That the birds call the winds, not Dragon Herald?

Tu Fu wrote this poem and the next in 764 at Ch'eng-tu (the
Brocade City), where he had met both Secretary Wei Feng
and the artist Ts'ao Pa. The latter's generalship was only
honorary, like a knighthood, bestowed for his service as a
painter chiefly of horses and of portraits at the court of the
Glorious Monarch. But his manner, poetic rather than
accurate in draughtsmanship, was by now unfashionable and
he himself old and poor. The poem was therefore probably
written as much to please him, like the next which is addressed
to him, as to please the owner of the painting 'Nine Horses'.
This painting unfortunately is long lost, like almost all
original T'ang painting; but it was seen and praised in a poem
by the great Su Tung-p'o in the eleventh century. (Nothing
at all seems now to be known of the work of the Prince
mentioned in the second line, who lived about a century
earlier.)
    The Glorious Monarch's 'White-at-Night charger' is the
subject of a famous painting, according to an inscription on it,
reproduced in photogravure in *A Short History of Chinese Art*
by Michael Sullivan (Faber Paperback, 1967); which also has
a full reproduction of 'The Glorious Monarch's Flight to Shu'
('Ming Huang's Journey . . .'). There is a colour reproduction
of the 'White-at-Night' painting in *Chinese Painting* by Peter
C. Swann (Éditions Pierre Tisné, Paris, 1958; English edition,

Zwemmer), who points out that the traditional ascription to Han Kan (see next poem) could hardly be true, on stylistic grounds comparing it with other of Han Kan's surviving works. Possibly (who knows?) this, though much restored, might have been Ts'ao Pa's painting itself.

The painting of the 'Nine Horses' seems to have been quite a recent work, because of the mention of 'Dappled Lion'; the horse presented by the Emperor to a famous General Kuo Tzu-i (A.D. 697–781) for his part in defeating the An Lu-shan rebellion. The other horse mentioned by name among the nine is 'Curly Piebald'; which was a famous charger of the Emperor T'ai-tsung (b. A.D. 597, reigned 627–49), and of which a portrait in stone-relief survives. (It may, of course, have been no more than Tu Fu's own imagination and love of history that made these identifications.)

Dragon Pool denotes the Court, being an artificial lake in the Imperial Gardens (not in the same park as the Serpentine). The presentation of the agate trencher was by the Emperor himself, for whom the painter then did the ritual dance of obeisance.

The fourth verse is a sort of *scherzo*, referring to a well-known Chinese 'family story': Chih Tun (A.D. 314–66) was a Buddhist monk and divine who managed, like a sporting parson, to keep a stable of splendid horses. When asked if this was really suitable to a man of his cloth, he answered that their Spirituality was an inspiration to him.

There follows the change of mood so often to be found in the conclusions of Tu Fu's poems. These last sad lines refer to the passing of the happier days of the Glorious Monarch's reign and to his death. They are packed with strongly charged poetic allusions; yet, as in all the best poetry, can also mysteriously go straight to the heart without the need for unravelling them all.

Kingfisher blue was an imperial colour; paying Tribute to Father River refers by means of a poetic allusion to the Glorious Monarch's death in 762; shooting dragons from river waters, besides being another poetic allusion, may refer to a peacetime sport of shooting at horse-drawn kites from barges; Golden Granary was a hill outside the capital, where the treasuries of grain and gold were and where the Glorious Monarch was buried; whilst Dragon Herald was a famous supernatural horse, here symbolizing the power, glory and gaiety of his vanished reign.

In form and in much of its style, despite its erudition, this poem is modelled on popular heroic ballads; as is the next and the poem about the ballet on p. 231. The adaptation of this form to artistic rather than military heroes was an invention of Tu Fu's own: a new and delightful kind of art criticism.

A SONG OF PAINTING:
FOR GENERAL TS'AO PA

O, General, you who hold
    Ts'ao Ts'ao's blood in you,
Now your threshold is cold,
    poorest commoner:

Yet his art is like gold
    untarnished in you,
Though his armies of old
    are long forgotten!

In your calligraphy, Lady Wei's student,
To outshine General Wang was your ambition;
Once painting, unaware of age's advent,
You have let (as if clouds) riches float by you.

When the Late Emperor called you to Audience,
Commissioned you to mount the Halls of Fragrance
To the faded Worthies of Cool Mist Gallery,
You, General, with your brush, revived a countenance
Or the cap on the head of a great Premier
Or, at fierce Marshal's waist, his arrow feathers:
So Duke Pao and Duke Ô once again bristled
But their forbidding gaze seemed gay with battle!

Artists to do the Steed, the 'Jade Flower Dapple',
As many as the hills, had failed in likeness
Till that day he was led below the Red Terrace
And brought up to its Gates the far winds with him:
You, General, on Command, spread silk before you
And you pondered awhile, planning painfully –
In a flash he appeared, born of Nine Dragons,
At once clearing the mind of common horses!

There were then two 'Jade Flowers', proudly at
    throneside,
At throneside and below, facing each other;
And august was the smile on purse presented,
The grooms and stable boys standing dumbfounded!
(Since your pupil Han Kan 'entered the chamber',
He too can paint horses, from every aspect;
Only Kan paints the flesh, not the strong structure,
With restraint that would make Hua-liu spiritless.)

You, General, paint so well, for you have Spirit:
When you met men of worth, painted truth of them;
So since you've had to steer through shields and lances
And portray everyone found by the roadside,
It is *you* who endure the sidelong glances . . .

Prince, though never since Time was man so beggared,
Only look, men of old whose names are famous
At last were frustrated, in body fettered!

'Threshold is cold' means that few came to his door.

Ts'ao Ts'ao (A.D. 155–220), Ts'ao Pa's ancestor, was one of
the great heroes (or in popular story and drama, villains) of
the time of the collapse and division of the Han Empire, the
period in Chinese history known as the Three Kingdoms,
which has a place in literature something like the Wars of the
Roses in ours. Ts'ao Ts'ao is famous for his huge armies (said
to have numbered more than a million men) and his ferocity,
including the ferocity of his discipline to his own men; under
which he once sentenced himself to death for letting his horse
stray in standing crops (but was persuaded to commute the
sentence). He was the arch-enemy of Chu-ko Liang, usually
the hero of the stories and the faithful and resourceful Minister
of the King of Shu. This Minister, popularly known as K'ung-
ming, meaning 'Enlightened by Confucius', was a special hero

of Tu Fu's and is the subject of the next two poems. However, the historic Ts'ao Ts'ao, founder of the Kingdom of Wei, was not merely the cruel and treacherous creature of later popular legend, but besides being a great leader, was also a renowned poet, painter and calligrapher; and the father of one of China's greatest poets, Ts'ao Chih (A.D. 192–232).

The Lady Wei (d. A.D. 140), a famous early calligrapher, is said to have inspired Brigadier-General Wang Hsi-chih (A.D. 321–79), the General Wang of the poem. He was a real general and became by common consent the greatest Chinese calligrapher of all time, and the virtual creator of the modern handwritten and printed forms of the characters. It was said of him that his writing was 'as light as floating clouds and as vigorous as a startled dragon'.

Having made this lofty comparison for the old painter, Tu Fu flies even higher by quoting Confucius; who 'unaware of age's advent, let, as if clouds, riches float by him'; and, again later, who let his disciples 'enter the (inner) chamber' of his wisdom. Such flattery was half gay, and not intended or likely to be taken entirely seriously: it was part of the very carefully concocted mixture (friendship to the Chinese has always been a cultivated art) made up of humour, sincere admiration and condolence which Tu Fu, as a poet and spiritual doctor, compounded for the old man. This is the greatest charm of his poem.

The Worthies whose portraits hung in the Cool Mist Gallery were those who had assisted the foundation of the dynasty about a century and a half earlier: Duke Pao and Duke Ô among them, who received these titles for their service. 'Jade Flower Dapple' was another famous horse belonging to the Glorious Monarch. The Nine Dragons were the Muses. (This is also the translation of the name, whether appropriate or not, of the city of Kowloon.)

Han Kan is mentioned in the notes to the preceding poem. 'Painting horses from every aspect' may well refer to his skill in new developments of shading and perspective, which were part of the new movement in art at that time. Han Kan's reputation, unlike Ts'ao Pa's, was to last to the present day. There are many stories about him, such as of a time when the Emperor asked him where he learnt to paint horses so well, and he replied: 'In Your Majesty's stables'; while Su Tung-p'o (see previous note) said of him, that when he painted horses he *was* a horse. Although the poor view of him expressed by Tu Fu may simply be part of the prescription, it sounds more sincere: 'Kan [his personal name] paints the flesh, not the bone' is the literal translation, but 'bone' does not refer to our notions of anatomy in painting; rather it is a term used of calligraphy as well as painting, and indeed applicable to poetry and all the arts including cooking which may be its ultimate origin. A proper balance between 'flesh' and 'bone', soft and hard, is like a proper balance between the Yin and the Yang, which the poet evidently thought lacking in Han Kan's work.

Hua-liu is the word for a bright bay horse with black points, but here is the name of one of the Heavenly Horses of the Duke of Mu (who succeeded as fifth sovereign of the Chou dynasty in 1001 B.C.) by the aid of which he was believed to have made lightning journeys all over the world. If Tu Fu had no dislike of Han Kan's style, he seems to have been unnecessarily rude. I think, however, that he may imply more than at first sight appears, by his allusion to a Heavenly Horse of the Duke of Mu. The third great Taoist book (it must not be supposed that Tu Fu, though called a 'Confucian', was unappreciative of such books), after the *Tao Te Ching* (see p. 154) and *Chuang Chou* (see Introduction, p. 36), is *Lieh Tzu.** In this there is a story of the Duke of Mu and of his legendary adviser on horses, Po Lo (Uncle Happy). The Duke said to Po Lo one day: 'You are getting very old. Is there anyone in your family who could find me a horse?' (Such posts were usually hereditary at that time.) Po Lo replied: 'To find a good horse, you must look at its shape, conformation, muscle and bone; but to find a Heavenly Horse, you must forget all these things. My sons are of the lesser talent: they could find you a good horse, but not a Heavenly Horse.

*Translated by A. C. Graham (John Murray, 1960).

There's an old man I know, who is a carrier of vegetables and firewood: he knows as much about horses as I ever did; please see him.'

The Duke saw this old man, who went away and after three months returned, saying 'I've found it!' The Duke said: 'What sort of horse is it?' and the old man replied 'A dun mare.' The Duke asked for it to be led in. The horse was a stallion and black. The Duke was not pleased and called for Po Lo: 'This man you sent me can't even tell the colour or the sex of a horse! How could you say he was a man who knew all about horses?'

Po Lo sighed deeply: *'Oh, is he as good as that now?'*

Taoist philosophy often expressed itself (like Zen Buddhism that followed it) in paradoxical jokes like this; but *Lieh Tzu* makes Po Lo go on to say, though not in the same words as Tu Fu's poem, that it was only the Spirit and Divine Mechanism that the old carrier had looked at in the horse, which of course proved to be a Heavenly one; and makes him end the parable with the splendid remark: 'It is as if, when he looks at a horse, there are more important things to him than horses!'

'Shields and lances', a phrase still current, refers to the state of war and disorder which continued after the An Lu-shan Rebellion. Tu Fu blames Ts'ao Pa's loss of reputation as a portraitist on the mean faces of the times.

The 'envoy' of this poem is strangely reminiscent of later European 'ballades'.

孔明廟前有老柏柯如青銅根如石霜皮溜雨四十圍黛色參天二千尺君臣已與時際會樹木猶爲人愛惜雲來氣接巫峽長月出寒通雪山白憶昨路繞錦亭東先主武侯同閟宮崔

THE BALLAD OF THE
ANCIENT CYPRESS

In front of K'ung-ming Shrine
    stands an old cypress,
With branches like green bronze
    and roots like granite;

Its hoary bark, far round,
    glistens with raindrops,
And blueblack hues, high up,
    blend in with Heaven's:

Long ago Statesman, King
    kept Time's appointment,
But still this standing tree
    has men's devotion;

United with the mists
    of ghostly gorges,
Through which the moon brings cold
    from snowy mountains.

(I recall near my hut
    on Brocade River
Another Shrine is shared
    by King and Statesman

On civil, ancient plains
    with stately cypress:
The paint there now is dim,
    windows shutterless . . .)

Wide, wide though writhing roots
    maintain its station,
Far, far in lonely heights,
    many's the tempest

When its hold is the strength
   of Divine Wisdom
And straightness by the work
   of the Creator . . .

Yet if a crumbling Hall
   needed a rooftree,
Yoked herds would, turning heads,
   balk at this mountain:

By art still unexposed
   all have admired it;
But axe though not refused,
   who could transport it?

How can its bitter core
   deny ants lodging,
All the while scented boughs
   give Phoenix housing?

Oh, ambitious unknowns,
   sigh no more sadly:
Using timber as big
   was never easy!

Tu Fu moved away from Ch'eng-tu in 765, on the death of
his patron there; and in 766 visited K'uei-chou or 'White
King' city (see Li Po's poem on p. 116), where he wrote this
and the next poem among many others in a particularly
productive period of his life. Technically, this poem seems to
have been a quite new invention of his: making a synthesis of
the ballad and the sonnet form in order to create a stately
combination of an heroic with a nature poem, as a political
allegory for the times. The two subjects of the poem, the
portrait of the great tree and the political meaning, are as
perfectly integrated as the two forms of poem themselves.

As to these forms, the tones, though producing fairly regular patterns a t times in the sonnet fashion, are mainly free, allowing kinds of expression by the aid of repetitions of the same tone (a feature in much of Li Po's poetry) that the sonnet patterns would not permit: for instance, in the second half of the first verse, translated as 'With branches like green bronze/ and roots like granite', in which there are six tense tones in succession, followed by a harsh-sounding word ending in -k.

In the matter of rhyme, however, and verbal parallelism, the sonnet form is strictly adhered to in such a way that, as far as these features alone are concerned, the poem is made up of three successive perfect sonnets. The rhyme is, of course, lost altogether in translation; but it is such that the lines in the translation ending 'cypress', 'granite', 'Heaven's', 'devotion' and 'mountains' all rhyme; there is a change of rhyme covering the lines in the translation ending 'River', 'Statesman', 'shutterless', 'tempest' and 'Creator'; and a further change of rhyme covering the lines ending 'rooftree', 'mountain', 'transport it', 'housing' and 'easy'. True to the form of three successive sonnets, the second and third verses (couplets in the original), the sixth and seventh verses, and the tenth and eleventh verses observe the rule of obligatory verbal parallelism; while the fourth and eighth verses have voluntary verbal parallelism, just as they might in sonnets: eight out of the twelve verses thus have this artifice; yet the whole poem seems as natural as it should be to suit its subject.

It is an extraordinary technical *tour de force*, but matched in quality by the content of the poem and its use of words: for example, 'Hall' in the ninth verse is a similar looking and sounding character to that for the name of the legendary first dynasty, the Hsia dynasty with traditional dates from 2205 to 1818 B.C.; while Great Hsia, that is the 'great Hall' here, is an old poetic name for China. This sort of thing might be cleverness to a fault, if it did not succeed in its object, at the same time becoming barely noticeable. Tu Fu has used all these means to make the two themes of the poem, physical and allegorical, seem to be one and indivisible.

Such a perfect blending might in itself be called perfect allegory, but there is more to it than that: the ancient Chinese philosophers, to an extent that Western philosophy would find a fault (and that has often led Chinese philosophy to seem scarcely reputable in Western eyes), failed to make a clear distinction between natural philosophy and moral philosophy. Instead, what distinction needed to be made was made by the opposite approaches of the Confucians and the Taoists to the same Way; which was the Way both of the natural universe and of human morality, the existence of which they equally accepted (see Introduction). What Tu Fu was doing, with all the poetic skills available to him, was seeking and celebrating this Way. His exercise in making the poem was therefore, in the Confucian tradition, a profoundly spiritual one; even though it may not all seem very like a 'religious poem'. (To many people a great deal of Chinese writing more directly religious than this would hardly seem to be so; largely because the factor of a sense of guilt is absent and the factor of a sense of humour is present.)

The K'ung-ming Shrine was dedicated to Chu-ko Liang (A.D. 181–234; see also note on Ts'ao Ts'ao, p. 21⅓); and was placed near the ancient cypress of the poem, because this was believed to have been planted by his own hand in the third century. Chu-ko Liang is the Statesman of the third verse, and served the King of Shu (Szechwan) as the supposed legitimate heir of the fallen Han dynasty (whose surname was Liu like his, though his claims to imperial blood were dubious). Chu-ko Liang was thought by Tu Fu to be the mode of the man needed to save the T'ang Empire of his own day: the Chinese ideal hero, who was always a reluctant statesman 'or general, if it was a matter of war: Chu-ko Liang was both); who was only with difficulty persuaded to leave his hermitage in the mountains and his books; and who, task completed, insisted on going back to them. The King of Shu had had to pay 'Three Calls at the Thatched Cottage' (a favourite subject of Chinese paintings) in person before he succeeded in persuading Chu-ko Liang, himself recorded as a painter of distinction, to leave the pleasures of art and scholarship and help him to win the Empire.

Although the King of Shu never succeeded in winning it, and the Empire remained divided for four centuries, Chu-ko Liang's loyalty and resourcefulness became legendary: in resourcefulness he is a kind of Chinese Ulysses. One story is of a time when he promised to make 100,000 arrows for a battle against Ts'ao Ts'ao in four days' time: the first day he did nothing; the second day he did nothing; the third day he did nothing until the evening when he loaded some bales of straw on ships, together with a few men below decks, and musical instruments. That night, which was foggy, his ships sailed into Ts'ao Ts'ao's fleet, making a fearful noise with the instruments; while Chu-ko Liang sat in the cabin of one of them, enjoying his wine. Then they sailed home, having, as he put it, 'borrowed 100,000 arrows from Ts'ao Ts'ao'! Because of his reputation, Chu-ko Liang became credited with inventions which were really prior to his own day: one of interest to mention being his use of the wheelbarrow to transport military equipment; a simple enough seeming invention but one that did not appear in the West till about a thousand years after Chu-ko Liang's own time.*

These two examples, though there could be countless others, of Chu-ko Liang's reputed genius may seem to be moving rather far from the poem; but they may serve to illustrate that the good Confucian hero was also what we might call diabolically clever. The preferred kind of cleverness for him was in making some very simple use of nature (Ts'ao Ts'ao's nature, the wheel as a fulcrum); which others, further removed from it, would not think of: '... its hold is the strength of Divine wisdom and straightness by the work of the Creator', as the poem says. (For 'the Creator', see the note on p. 159.)

'By art still unexposed' is one of these phrases in Tu Fu, and in Chinese poetry generally, capable of receiving a great many

*See Needham, *Science and Civilisation in China*, Vol. IV, Pt 2, Section 27 (Cambridge University Press, 1965).

relevant meanings: for the tree, for instance, it can mean 'un-carved' ('the uncarved block' is a special Taoist term for natural perfection); and for the statesman (or 'ambitious un-known') it can mean 'without having had the opportunity to show *his* art' in statesmanship or literature – the Confucians did not make a clear distinction between the two.

The Phoenix is, of course, the Bird of Inspiration: it is, with the Chinese as with us, a bird of fire (although the Chinese do not have all our legends associated with it, such as its rising from its ashes); it is the creature, *par excellence*, of the Yang; and it has in its plumage the original Five Colours of painting and in its voice the original Five Notes of music. As David Hawkes observes, the phoenix had a special meaning for Tu Fu, who frequently used it as his own symbol. The very first childish attempt at a poem in his notebooks (now, of course, themselves long lost)* which he kept so carefully in his life-time, adding poem to poem, was written at the age of six and was probably inspired by hearing grown-ups refer to 'the Phoenix Song' sung by the Madman of Ch'u to Confucius, contemptuously warning him against political ambition. (The Madman of Ch'u was a character with something in common with the 'old angler' in Li Po's poem on p. 139.) Tu Fu's little poem went:

> Now I am six
> I feel very strong
> And open my mouth
> With a Phoenix Song!

In the same verse as the phoenix, the ants (in the original, 'mole-crickets and ants') also have an ancestry: in the Book of Chuang Chou (see Li Po's poem on p. 141) it is said that 'the Great Fish, once out of its water, is a prey to the mole-crickets and ants'. The implication, of course, is partly that the 'timber', for not being used as the Creator intended, is 'like a fish out of

---

*They would have been in the form of scrolls, which 'books' in a poem such as that on p. 199 also means. In China it was the invention of printing in the ninth and tenth centuries that led to the use of books as we know them.

water'; but the allusion is so lightly touched that it seems excessive to make it explicit, and it might be said to be somewhere between a 'literary allusion' and 'borrowed diction'. The Chinese word for 'timber' itself, in the last verse, is exactly the same in sound and etymology (the root meaning being 'what is available') as the word for 'talent'; which is much used in a particular collective and abstract sense of 'the talent available to assist the government of the Empire'.

But by now, in the last verse, Tu Fu makes it seem that he has become conscious of beginning to identify the great tree with himself; and he ends the poem with a lightness, a suggestion even of colloquialism in the original, that shows him laughing at himself and releases the tension of the poem – a very typical touch.

THE EIGHT FORMATIONS

Glory outlasting the Kingdoms divided in Three,
The Fame achieved by this military Figure of Eight:
The running river leaves these stones unmoved,
By-passing sorrow at failing to swallow Wu!

This epigram was written in 766, at about the same time as
'The Ancient Cypress' and also at White King, near which
there were some great stones in the Yangtse and on its shore,
perhaps megaliths from very early times. These were popularly
thought (and apparently also by Tu Fu) to have been put
there by Chu-ko Liang in order to demonstrate the famous
tactical dispositions by which he had won many battles – the
stones were in fact known as 'The Eight Formations'. Like the
wheelbarrow, it seems that these tactics were also an invention
from before Chu-ko Liang's own time; though he may have
improved on them, and they have always since been associated
with his name.

The Three Kingdoms were Shu, Wei and Wu. The King-
dom of Shu once made an onslaught disastrous to itself
against Wu. Tu Fu, who was an inveterate sightseer and con-
templator of ancient and natural monuments, meditates upon
the transitoriness of all human endeavour, even his great hero's,
and upon the waters in the river that 'all Eastward flow'. The
original epigram is in only twenty syllables, in the five-
syllable metre that is usually translated by nine in this book.

FROM A HEIGHT

The winds cut, clouds are high,
  apes wail their sorrows,
The ait is fresh, sand white,
  birds fly in circles;

On all sides fallen leaves
  go rustling, rustling,
While ceaseless river waves
  come rippling, rippling:

Autumn's each faded mile
  seems like my journey
To mount, alone and ill,
  to this balcony;

Life's failures and regrets
  frosting my temples,
And wretched that I've had
  to give up drinking.

This sonnet is dated by Tu Fu himself as written on the
'Double Ninth', the ninth day of the ninth month, which
would be 6 October 767. It was evidently written on another
Yangtse River voyage, somewhere near White King. (He
spent most of the rest of his life, already wasting from con-
sumption, on such voyages; and died on one.)

In this poem, his boat had probably stopped for the passen-
gers to have refreshments at some river island, the 'ait'; and
Tu Fu, perhaps because he was unable to drink wine, left the
party and climbed alone to the balcony of a belvedere.

Although he was a very sick man, probably by now the
skin and bone of many representations of him in imaginary
portraits, and although he had reason now to be bitterly dis-
appointed in his ambitions, his cry of complaint manages to
be at once naturally beautiful, dignified and humorous.

The humour, to our canons of taste, may even come as something of a shock; as if we had been foolishly mistaken at first in thinking this a sadly beautiful poem, and should quickly re-categorize it as a humorous one. But these are not categories that Tu Fu or other Chinese poets of the time would have thought of distinguishing in relation to it. As David Hawkes very finely says:

The magnificent sorrow of this threnody for dying nature ends with Tu Fu's remark that he has had to give up drinking . . . it is hard not to find this ending uncomfortable. Yet Tu Fu does this sort of thing so often that one must look for something other than mere neurotic self-pity if one is to reach any sort of understanding with him at all.

My own view is that Tu Fu's famous compassion in fact includes himself, viewed quite objectively and almost as an afterthought. We can perhaps understand this poem if we think of a typical Chinese landscape with a tiny figure in one corner of it looking at the view. In this poem the little figure is Tu Fu himself, who, far from solipsistically shrinking the landscape to his own dimensions, lends grandeur to it by contrasting it with his own slightly comical triviality.

The thought of Tu Fu's 'famous compassion' including himself, as something quite different from self-pity (of which, as said in the Introduction, he was singularly free), seems a very perceptive one. It is Tu Fu's particular quality that, although he is a Confucian and might (unlike Li Po) be called a 'moralist', his compassion is never morally selective: witness his compassion for Yang Kuei-fei in 'Lament by the Riverside'.

BALLAD ON SEEING
A PUPIL OF THE LADY KUNG-SUN
DANCE THE SWORD MIME

On the 19th day of the Tenth Month of Year II of Ta-li (15 November 767), I saw the Lady Li, Twelfth, of Lin-ying dance the Mime of the Sword at the Residence of Lieutenant-Governor Yüan Ch'i of K'uei Chou Prefecture; and both the subtlety of her interpretation and her virtuosity on points so impressed me that I asked of her, who had been her Teacher? She replied: 'I was a Pupil of the great Lady Kung-sun!'

In Year V of K'ai-yüan (A.D. 717), when I was no more than a tiny boy, I remember being taken in Yü-yen City to see Kung-sun dance both this Mime and 'The Astrakhan Hat'.

For her combination of flowing rhythms with vigorous attack, Kung-sun had stood alone even in an outstanding epoch. No member at all of the *corps de ballet*, of any rank whatever, either of the Sweet Springtime Garden or of the Pear Garden Schools, could interpret such dances as she could; throughout the reign of His Late Majesty, Saintly in Peace and Godlike in War! But where now is that jadelike face, where are those brocade costumes? And I whiteheaded! And her Pupil here, too, no longer young!

Having learned of this Lady's background, I came to realize that she had, in fact, been reproducing faithfully all the movements, all the little gestures, of her Teacher; and I was so stirred by that memory, that I decided to make a Ballad of the Mime of the Sword.

There was a time when the great calligrapher, Chang Hsü of Wu, famous for his wild running hand, had

昔有佳人公孫氏一舞劍器
動四方觀者如山色沮喪天
地為之久低昂㸌如羿射
九日落矯如羣帝驂龍翔來
如雷霆收震怒罷如江海凝
清光絳脣珠袖兩寂寞晚

several opportunities of watching the Lady Kung-sun
dance this Sword Mime (as it is danced in Turkestan);
and he discovered, to his immense delight, that doing
so had resulted in marked improvement in his own
calligraphic art! From *that*, know the Lady Kung-sun!

A Great Dancer there was,
    the Lady Kung-sun,
And her 'Mime of the Sword'
    made the World marvel!

Those, many as the hills,
    who had watched breathless
Thought sky and earth themselves
    moved to her rhythms:

As she flashed, the Nine Suns
    fell to the Archer;
She flew, was a Sky God
    on saddled dragon;

She came on, the pent storm
    before it thunders;
And she ceased, the cold light
    off frozen rivers!

Her red lips and pearl sleeves
    are long since resting,
But a dancer revives
    of late their fragrance:

The Lady of Lin-ying
    in White King city
Did the piece with such grace
    and lively spirit

That I asked! Her reply
  gave the good reason
And we thought of those times
  with deepening sadness:

There had waited at Court
  eight thousand Ladies
(With Ḳung-sun, from the first,
  chief at the Sword Dance);

And fifty years had passed
  (a palm turned downward)
While the winds, bringing dust,
  darkened the Palace

And they scattered like mist
  those in Pear Garden,
On whose visages still
  its sun shines bleakly!

*

But now trees had clasped hands
  at Golden Granary
And grass played its sad tunes
  on Ch'ü-t'ang's Ramparts,

For the swift pipes had ceased
  playing to tortoiseshell;
The moon rose in the East,
  joy brought great sorrow:

                An old man knows no more
                   where he is going;
                On these wild hills, footsore,
                   he will not hurry!

Tu Fu celebrates the work of a fine though ageing ballerina,
seen at White King city in the Yangtse Gorges when he was
on one of his river tours, by means of the heroic ballad form
which he had used to celebrate the work of the old painter in
the poems on pp. 209 and 213.

He gives the date of her performance in his prose introduc-
tion to the ballad; but the date of '717' for his being taken to
see the great Lady Kung-sun herself results from an emendation
of the usual text: this has '715', which would be K'ai-yüan III,
a 3 and a 5 being easily confused in rapid Chinese handwriting.
The emendation makes the little Tu Fu five instead of three
years old, which is much more probable; and would be
exactly fifty years earlier, as he says in the ballad.

For drama, the beginning in China was the Yüan (Mongol)
dynasty, 1280–1368;* it does not seem to have existed as such
in the T'ang dynasty when the arts of the theatre were ballet,
song and mime. From descriptions of this dance which Tu Fu
saw, it was a solo danced without any 'props' (thus there was
no sword in the ballerina's bare hands, but she mimed it);
while she is said to have worn a martial, male costume. Tu Fu
is therefore thinking of Kung-sun herself and how she usually
looked, as a ballerina rather than in this particular piece, when
he remembers her 'red lips and pearl sleeves'. Tu Fu says the
piece was danced in the style of 'West of the Yangtse' (trans-
lated as 'Turkestan'), and it was probably at its climax ex-
tremely fast and vigorous, much like Tartar or so-called
Polovtsian dances known today through Russian ballet. 'The
Astrakhan Hat' is likely to have been similar. None of the
calligraphy of the 'mad monk' Chang Hsü of Wu, though

---

*See *Six Yuan Plays*, translated by Liu Jung-en (Penguin Books,
1972).

among the most famous of its day, survives; but there is calligraphy by a contemporary, probably Huai-su, in much the same style, of 'grass' or 'rough draft' shorthand – a style in which Chairman Mao excels today. Huai-su's wild calligraphy seems to give an impression of what the Lady Kungsun's dancing must have been like.* (The Chinese art of calligraphy in all its styles is closely related to the art of ballet; as indeed is the Chinese art of poetry.)

The Sweet Springtime Garden was the name of the park with the Serpentine, in 'Lament by the Riverside': it seems there was a ballet school there with a particular style. The Pear Garden survives today as a name for a theatre, or for 'the theatre' as an art and profession: it was established by the Glorious Monarch himself, in a pear orchard inside the Forbidden Garden of the Imperial Palace, as a school of music and dancing with 300 students. (Tu Fu's 'eight thousand ladies' in the ballad elicits from an old Chinese commentator: 'What a glorious exaggeration!') In this part of the prose preface Tu Fu goes into some technicalities of the organization of the *corps de ballet*, rather like a journalist and apparently getting it all rather wrong: these technicalities have been omitted. David Hawkes suggests, with great probability, that there was a sad irony now in Tu Fu's reference to the Glorious Monarch as 'Saintly in Peace and Godlike in War'.

In the ballad itself, 'the Nine Suns fell to the Archer' long ago, when there rose ten suns in the heavens and they scorched all the earth until a god called the Great Archer took his bow and shot nine of them down.

Although it is difficult to be sure, without personal

* Two specimens of this may be found in *Chinese Calligraphers and their Art* by Ch'en Chih-mai, Melbourne University Press; with an entertaining account of Chang Hsü himself, who 'in moments of extreme wildness even tried to write with his head, soaking his hair in a basin of ink, twisting and turning his neck against the blank wall. But we have good reason to believe that he was a most accomplished artist, even when he was sober.' (The poem ascribed to Li Po there, however, seems to be a forgery based on this one, which was written after Li Po's death.)

234

pronouns, I think that Tu Fu's conversation with the ballerina, the Lady of Lin-ying, was not confined to question and answer, but continued (so, '*we* thought of those times'); that the lines in parenthesis are her contributions, she making the ballet gesture of a palm turned downward for the passage of time when he says that fifty years have passed; and that he is looking at her face at the end of their conversation.

Golden Granary, where the Glorious Monarch was buried outside Ch'ang-an (he had died in 762), has already been mentioned at the end of the poem on p. 210 and in its note. Ch'ü-t'ang is the Yangtse gorge, near White King, in the fifth verse of Li Po's 'Ballad of Ch'ang-kan' (p. 125). The 'Ramparts' might refer to the sides of the gorge, or be the walled city of White King itself referred to thus in a kenning; but as usual in such cases in Chinese poetry, it can probably be said to be a bit of both. Ch'ang-an and White King (K'uei-chou) are far apart, so that this verse is like saying: 'Now trees have clasped hands at Windsor Great Park, and grass plays its sad tunes on Edin's Ramparts'; indicating the melancholy that Tu Fu imagines as falling over the whole of China. But he imagines this on the ceasing of the music of 'the swift pipes' he has been listening to while watching the dancing, now, and not as part of what went before the asterisk I have inserted. These sudden shifts of space and time are common in Chinese poetry; and sometimes disconcerting to us, accustomed as we are to logical nexus.

'Playing to tortoiseshell' is abbreviated in the translation ('tortoiseshell' being a long word, but essential to retain) from 'playing to tortoiseshell-bordered mats'. The Chinese in T'ang times sat on mats on the floor at banquets, where such ballets were staged, like the Japanese of today; who retain much of earlier Chinese customs and dress. Tortoiseshell-bordered mats were very grand.

These lines win from the old Chinese commentator already quoted: 'Surely a god was guiding his brush when he wrote this!' The magic, I think, is partly in the 'visual rhyme' of 'tortoiseshell' with 'the moon rose in the East': much as one might speak of the 'visual rhyme' in 'I'll hang my harp on a weeping willow tree'. 'Joy brings the greatest sorrow' is a proverb. This might have some kind of allusion to Yang Kuei-fei, at one level, but seems chiefly to evoke, together with the last verse, a well-known 'after theatre' feeling everyone has experienced after witnessing something especially moving. One has been to the ballet with Tu Fu in the eighth century.

By bent grasses
in a gentle wind
Under straight mast
I'm alone tonight,

And the stars hang
above the broad plain
But moon's afloat
in this Great River:

Oh, where's my name
among the poets?
Official rank?
'Retired for ill-health.'

Drifting, drifting,
what am I more than
A single gull
between sky and earth?

This sonnet was written on another of Tu Fu's voyages, in the spring of 768. The Great River is the usual Chinese name for the Yangtse. Tu Fu, later in his residence at Ch'eng-tu and until he left there in 765, had held a further, at least nominal official appointment: as (Consultant) Assistant-Secretary in the Ministry of Works. Despite the title of Tu Fu's appointment, his duties seem to have been rather as a military adviser to the Provincial Governor, on call; and perhaps not in reality very often called, but allowed to hold an official rank and receive a small salary. Now he was retired altogether.

He had had some name as a poet, in some quarters considerable, during his lifetime; but none such as his friend and hero, Li Po, and others had enjoyed. Now friends and patrons had died, he was finally out of official life, and so inevitably largely

removed from Society of that day. Perhaps the third verse of
this may seem to come near to that self-pity which this book
has denied he possessed; but the poem seems to have an
objectivity about it, especially in the last verse, which lifts it
above that and shows the serenity of his character maintained;
as it seems to be, in a different way, in the next poem.

从

ts'ung

to follow; *hence* sequential, from
(character shows one man
following another)

[see overleaf]

客從

客從南溟來　遺我泉客珠　珠中有隱字
欲辯不成書　緘之篋笥久　以俟公家須
開視化為血　哀今徵斂無

FROM THE SOUTH SEA

From the South Sea
did a Guest appear
And give to me
a Mermaid's tear

And in that Pearl
there were cloudy signs:
I tried to unfurl
what lay in those lines;

Wrapped it away
in a little box,
Kept it to pay
the Government Tax:

Opened and saw
it had turned to blood –
Alas, today
I have nothing else!

This was written in April 769, according to the commentator Ch'ou Chao-ao who says that it was inspired by a rise in taxes at that time, such as hit smallholders very hard. Tu Fu was himself now a smallholder, as his only source of income. Professor Denis Twitchett of Cambridge has very kindly given me the following information about this:

'In 768 the irregular money taxes on land ... were raised 50 per cent to meet a 20 per cent increase in official salaries. In 769 both summer and autumn collections of the regular land tax seem to have begun ... the entire structure of the household levy was revised, with the aim of bringing under taxation unregistered squatters who had fled to the south in the An Lu-shan disturbances, and also to impose taxes on urban dwellers. This is almost certainly the measure in question.'

I think that Tu Fu refers both to this measure and at the same time to the Pearl as his own inspiration which, like many artists, he felt he had failed to justify: a disappointment that pervades many of his last poems. The joining of such different subjects is typical of Chinese poetry, and of Tu Fu's in particular.

The poem is an affectionate parody of an ancient song from the Han dynasty, which began:

> From far away
> did a Guest appear
> And give to me
> a bolt of silk.
>
> So though he's gone
> a thousand miles,
> I know my Love's
> heart is still near!
>
> I'll broider it
> with a brace of ducks . . .

These were, of course, the Mandarin Ducks of conjugal fidelity; the 'Guest' in such songs being a distant lover's emissary. The word-order in the Chinese is such that the first line and title of both songs is 'A Guest (or Stranger) from . . .'. Tu Fu wrote two other poems with the same beginning but different provenances for the 'Guest', whom here he makes come from the 'South Sea' so that his distant lover may be a mermaid sending him a pearl, which in Chinese folklore was thought to be a mermaid's tear. (The old Han dynasty song continues into technicalities of bridal dressmaking beyond my powers to translate; but mentioning such familiar things as 'true lovers' knots', also making the 'long silk/longing thoughts' pun referred to in the note on Li Po's poem on p. 119.)

In this poem Tu Fu wrote something his rustic neighbours may well have been able to understand: indeed it seems probable that despite his own poverty, for a member of the official class, he wrote it as much, or more, on their behalf and for that reason in a folk style. Most of his poems were so concise and dependent on literary knowledge for their understanding as to have been meaningless to the illiterate. (The great poet Po Chü-i, born two years after Tu Fu's death, was to develop Wordsworthian theories about poetic language, and read some of his poems to an old illiterate countrywoman, altering what she could not understand.)

Much misunderstanding would otherwise arise among the illiterate because of the number of homophones in the language. William Hung has in the Notes to his book a charming story of how an admirer of Tu Fu, years after his death, raised a shrine to his memory; piously choosing his title of 'Reminder', from the time he was nearest to the Throne. To the peasantry this sounded like 'Tenth Aunt' in the Tu family; whom they duly adored and one day married with great ceremony to another local saint, male but who had come into existence in exactly the same way; so that the holy couple might live together (as they still seem to have done, centuries later) near their village, fruitfully conveying sympathetic magic to the crops.

ON MEETING LI KUEI-NIEN,
SOUTH OF THE RIVER

Often we used to meet in Prince Ch'i's Palace,
Or I would hear you sing at Ts'ui Chiu's Mansion:
How fair the scene is here, South of the River,
Where I meet you once more, the petals falling!

This is believed to be Tu Fu's last quatrain, written in the
autumn of 770. Li Kuei-nien had been a famous singer, teacher
of music and composer at the court of the Glorious Monarch.
He and his two brothers, also musicians, had in those days
made a fabulous fortune out of their art.

Tu Fu died, perhaps on the same river voyage, in November
770.

LIST OF TITLES

LI PO

TU FU

INDEX OF FIRST LINES

including poems by other poets

READ MORE IN PENGUIN

In every corner of the world, on every subject under the sun, Penguin represents quality and variety – the very best in publishing today.

For complete information about books available from Penguin – including Puffins, Penguin Classics and Arkana – and how to order them, write to us at the appropriate address below. Please note that for copyright reasons the selection of books varies from country to country.

In the United Kingdom: Please write to *Dept. EP, Penguin Books Ltd, Bath Road, Harmondsworth, West Drayton, Middlesex UB7 ODA*

In the United States: Please write to *Consumer Sales, Penguin USA, P.O. Box 999, Dept. 17109, Bergenfield, New Jersey 07621-0120.* VISA and MasterCard holders call 1-800-253-6476 to order Penguin titles

In Canada: Please write to *Penguin Books Canada Ltd, 10 Alcorn Avenue, Suite 300, Toronto, Ontario M4V 3B2*

In Australia: Please write to *Penguin Books Australia Ltd, P.O. Box 257, Ringwood, Victoria 3134*

In New Zealand: Please write to *Penguin Books (NZ) Ltd, Private Bag 102902, North Shore Mail Centre, Auckland 10*

In India: Please write to *Penguin Books India Pvt Ltd, 706 Eros Apartments, 56 Nehru Place, New Delhi 110 019*

In the Netherlands: Please write to *Penguin Books Netherlands bv, Postbus 3507, NL-1001 AH Amsterdam*

In Germany: Please write to *Penguin Books Deutschland GmbH, Metzlerstrasse 26, 60594 Frankfurt am Main*

In Spain: Please write to *Penguin Books S. A., Bravo Murillo 19, 1° B, 28015 Madrid*

In Italy: Please write to *Penguin Italia s.r.l., Via Felice Casati 20, I–20124 Milano*

In France: Please write to *Penguin France S. A., 17 rue Lejeune, F–31000 Toulouse*

In Japan: Please write to *Penguin Books Japan, Ishikiribashi Building, 2–5–4, Suido, Bunkyo-ku, Tokyo 112*

In Greece: Please write to *Penguin Hellas Ltd, Dimocritou 3, GR–106 71 Athens*

In South Africa: Please write to *Longman Penguin Southern Africa (Pty) Ltd, Private Bag X08, Bertsham 2013*

PENGUIN AUDIOBOOKS

A Quality of Writing that Speaks for Itself

Penguin Books has always led the field in quality publishing. Now you can listen at leisure to your favourite books, read to you by familiar voices from radio, stage and screen. Penguin Audiobooks are ideal as gifts, for when you are travelling or simply to enjoy at home. They are produced to an excellent standard, and abridgements are always faithful to the original texts. From thrillers to classic literature, biography to humour, with a wealth of titles in between, Penguin Audiobooks offer you quality, entertainment and the chance to rediscover the pleasure of listening.

You can order Penguin Audiobooks through Penguin Direct by telephoning (0181) 899 4036. The lines are open 24 hours every day. Ask for Penguin Direct, quoting your credit card details.

Published or forthcoming:

Emma by Jane Austen, read by Fiona Shaw

Persuasion by Jane Austen, read by Joanna David

Pride and Prejudice by Jane Austen, read by Geraldine McEwan

The Tenant of Wildfell Hall by Anne Brontë, read by Juliet Stevenson

Jane Eyre by Charlotte Brontë, read by Juliet Stevenson

Villette by Charlotte Brontë, read by Juliet Stevenson

Wuthering Heights by Emily Brontë, read by Juliet Stevenson

The Woman in White by Wilkie Collins, read by Nigel Anthony and Susan Jameson

Heart of Darkness by Joseph Conrad, read by David Threlfall

Tales from the One Thousand and One Nights, read by Souad Faress and Raad Rawi

Moll Flanders by Daniel Defoe, read by Frances Barber

Great Expectations by Charles Dickens, read by Hugh Laurie

Hard Times by Charles Dickens, read by Michael Pennington

Martin Chuzzlewit by Charles Dickens, read by John Wells

The Old Curiosity Shop by Charles Dickens, read by Alec McCowen

PENGUIN AUDIOBOOKS

Crime and Punishment by Fyodor Dostoyevsky, read by Alex Jennings

Middlemarch by George Eliot, read by Harriet Walter

Silas Marner by George Eliot, read by Tim Pigott-Smith

The Great Gatsby by F. Scott Fitzgerald, read by Marcus D'Amico

Madame Bovary by Gustave Flaubert, read by Claire Bloom

Jude the Obscure by Thomas Hardy, read by Samuel West

The Return of the Native by Thomas Hardy, read by Steven Pacey

Tess of the D'Urbervilles by Thomas Hardy, read by Eleanor Bron

The Iliad by Homer, read by Derek Jacobi

Dubliners by James Joyce, read by Gerard McSorley

The Dead and Other Stories by James Joyce, read by Gerard McSorley

On the Road by Jack Kerouac, read by David Carradine

Sons and Lovers by D. H. Lawrence, read by Paul Copley

The Fall of the House of Usher by Edgar Allan Poe, read by Andrew Sachs

Wide Sargasso Sea by Jean Rhys, read by Jane Lapotaire and Michael Kitchen

The Little Prince by Antoine de Saint-Exupéry, read by Michael Maloney

Frankenstein by Mary Shelley, read by Richard Pasco

Of Mice and Men by John Steinbeck, read by Gary Sinise

Travels with Charley by John Steinbeck, read by Gary Sinise

The Pearl by John Steinbeck, read by Hector Elizondo

Dr Jekyll and Mr Hyde by Robert Louis Stevenson, read by Jonathan Hyde

Kidnapped by Robert Louis Stevenson, read by Robbie Coltrane

The Age of Innocence by Edith Wharton, read by Kerry Shale

The Buccaneers by Edith Wharton, read by Dana Ivey

Mrs Dalloway by Virginia Woolf, read by Eileen Atkins

POEMS OF THE LATE T'ANG

Translated by A. C. Graham

Chinese poetry achieved an unsurpassed greatness in the eighth and ninth centuries A.D. Its most famous poets, from the widely established Tu Fu to Li Shangyin (one of the first of Chinese poets to make love his central theme), explore their language to its utmost limits in poems that have a sharp definition of outline and yet a complexity and allusiveness unknown to Western writers.

The seven poets of this anthology include Han Yu, who has the power, it is said, to create beauty out of ugliness and Li Ho, whose morbid sensitivity relates him to Baudelaire. The brilliant political allegory *The Eclipse* by Lu T'ung, the bold imagery of Meng Chiao, and the swift elegant poems of Tu Mu complete the volume.

LAO TZU · TAO TE CHING

Translated by D. C. Lau

The Lao Tzu as it is usually called, is the principal classic in the thought of Taoism. Traditionally ascribed to one Lao Tzu, an older contemporary of Confucius, the work is more probably an anthology of wise sayings compiled in about the fourth century B.C. As a treatise both on personal conduct and on government it is moral rather than mystical in tone, and advances a philosophy of meekness as the surest path to survival. In the clear English of D. C. Lau's new translation this famous Chinese book can be enjoyed especially for its pure poetry.

READ MORE IN PENGUIN

A CHOICE OF CLASSICS

Basho	**The Narrow Road to the Deep North**
	On Love and Barley
Cao Xueqin	**The Story of the Stone** also known as **The Dream of The Red Chamber** (in five volumes)
Confucius	**The Analects**
Khayyam	**The Ruba'iyat of Omar Khayyam**
Lao Tzu	**Tao Te Ching**
Li Po/Tu Fu	**Li Po and Tu Fu**
Sei Shonagon	**The Pillow Book of Sei Shonagon**
Wang Wei	**Poems**
Yuan Qu and Others	**The Songs of the South**

ANTHOLOGIES AND ANONYMOUS WORKS

The Bhagavad Gita
Buddhist Scriptures
The Dhammapada
Hindu Myths
The Koran
The Laws of Manu
New Songs from a Jade Terrace
The Rig Veda
Speaking of Siva
Tales from the Thousand and One Nights
The Upanishads